The Sporting Epicure

By the same author:

Going to the Moors (1979)

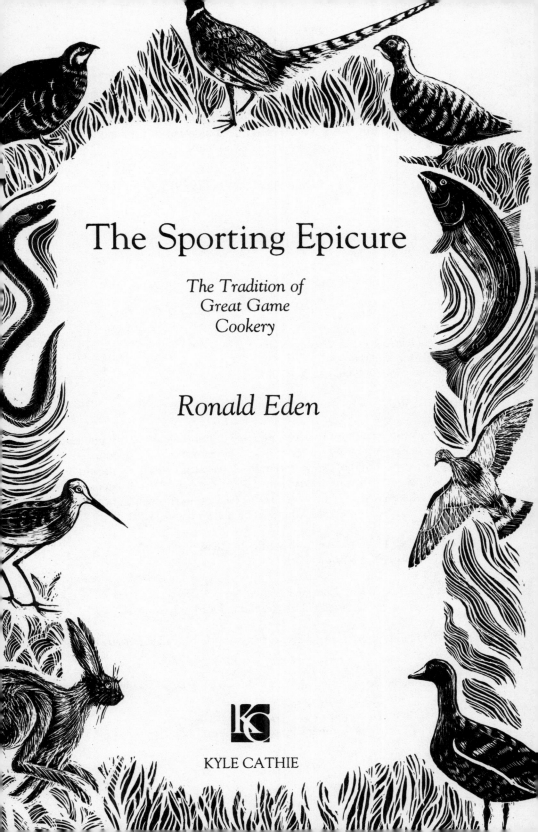

The Sporting Epicure

The Tradition of
Great Game
Cookery

Ronald Eden

KYLE CATHIE

Acknowledgement

I am especially indebted to Libby Weir-Breen, who not only typed the manuscript, but who made valuable suggestions and gave me great encouragement.

First published 1991 in Great Britain by
Kyle Cathie Limited
3 Vincent Square London SW1P 2LX

ISBN 1 85626 015 1

A Cataloguing in Publication record for this title is available from the British Library

Designed by Lorraine Abraham
Typeset by Rowland Phototypesetting Limited,
Bury St Edmunds, Suffolk.
Printed by Butler and Tanner Limited, Frome and London.

Contents

To Rosemary
who hates cooking but who cooks so well

Foreword

A TRADITION of good British cooking has been nurtured in country houses since the early Tudor era. Not of least importance in the libraries of houses great and small were the kitchen receipt books, carefully and proudly kept, with ideas included from other households. The produce of a farm or estate is wild as well as domestic, and therefore game featured prominently.

Ideas on the cookery of game were stimulated between the early 19th and 20th centuries when enthusiasm for field sports was reflected in the huge number of books published on shooting, stalking and fishing. Most notable was the Fur, Feather & Fin series, monographs published by Longmans, Green in the 1890s, each of which contains an essay on the cookery of the subject, written with unrivalled elegance. Many of the authors of this branch of literature were themselves sportsmen, who took an interest in their quarry from the field to the table. Their own practically acquired knowledge, combined with the collected recipes of their households, made them uniquely qualified to give advice on how game should be prepared and cooked.

The repertoire of game dishes was enhanced by the spread of the British Empire. One of the attractions of serving in overseas possessions was the sport that could be enjoyed, and soldiers and administrators brought home with them recipes from other nations which were then adapted for British climate and taste.

It has been said that the Empire was built on British beef, but although the British have had the reputation of being the biggest meat-eaters in Europe, game has never enjoyed the popularity continentals bestow on it. It may be more expensive than beef or lamb, but less so than it used to be. In recent years a particularly plentiful supply of venison and pheasants seems to have done little to stimulate demand.

This is not a cookery book; it is intended for the fireside or the bedside more than the side of the stove, but I hope it will quicken interest in game as well as give amusement and some instruction. My selection of quotations is personal and idiosyncratic; it does not attempt to be comprehensive, nor could it be. There are many good modern books devoted to game cookery, and it is not my purpose to try to emulate them. I have, however, resurrected ideas from old and much forgotten writers who are not as well known today as they should be.

The sporting authors I have included are mingled with the great domestic cookery writers such as Eliza Acton, Margaret Dods and Hannah Glasse. I have paid less heed to the dishes of Escoffier and other classical masters on the grounds that their preparations tend to be too elaborate for the home kitchen. On the choice of quotations I may be criticised for giving particular weight to a few authors such as H. B. C. Pollard, but I believe they hit the nail on the head so often that their views deserve emphasis.

Many writers contradict each other dogmatically on diverse matters, but that merely adds spice and readers will make their own judgement. On one matter I wish to express my own view, because it is an unpopular one. Young animals and birds are, of course, tenderer than old ones. The latter, however, have more flavour and there is no reason why they should necessarily be consigned to the stewpot. After hanging for a few days, dress them and put them in the deep freeze for three months. When you take them out and cook them they will compare very favourably with the young in tenderness, and flavour will be incomparably better.

I have not presumed to substitute the modern for the archaic in cooking methods and equipment; cooks and chefs will use their sophistication in bringing things up to date. I do wish, though, that cookery schools would spend some time in teaching their pupils elementary lessons in the preparation of game. As a sporting estate we bring our game into the larder in fur and feather. It has then, at one stage or another, to be drawn, hung for the requisite time, and finally plucked or skinned. Excellent though our chefs may be at cooking game, they have little knowledge of preparation because they have not been taught.

Breakfast

SMELL, the most evocative of senses, can capture memories in fine detail. The aroma that emanated at breakfast time from the Cromlix* dining room fifty years ago kindles a fond memory of warmth, comfort and an auspicious start to the day. It was an improbably delicious mixture of burning methylated spirit that heated the copper hotplates bearing the entrée dishes, fused with the tang of egg and bacon, tomatoes, sausages, grilled kidneys and kedgeree.

A year or so ago, a magazine article pronounced breakfasts at Cromlix to be as good as any in Britain, and worth travelling a long way to sample. In fact, we do no more than follow the precepts of our forebears, with some modifications. There is no longer a demand for devilled dishes, though they may be popular as a savoury for dinner, and therefore I have included examples. Other recipes are similarly interchangeable. What, for example, can excel a fried brown trout for breakfast, especially with an appetite sharpened by catching him an hour earlier on the dawn rise?

Another staple item of the old-fashioned sideboard, cold meat, is likewise out of favour. Ham, tongue, beef, pressed galantine of chicken and lobster, no longer have their place and I regret it. What a sight it all was.

As people are drawn to us, amongst other things, for our breakfasts, so in pre-war days would the heads of departments of the outdoor staff converge on the pantry at about ten o'clock. Excuses were easy enough to find. The gardener would bring flowers, fruit and vegetables, the gamekeeper game or rabbits for the dogs, and the forester logs and kindling for the fires. Their goods delivered, they would feast on the cornucopia of leftovers, conveniently removed from the dining room to

* Cromlix is my family home; the house, built in 1880, was turned into an hotel in 1981.

the back quarters. Nothing was wasted, and the perquisite of breakfast was one of many which made up, at least in some measure, for low wages and hard conditions of work.

On Marriage

Never marry a man who does not eat a good breakfast.

Rose Henniker Heaton, *The Perfect Hostess*, 1931

An Important Meal

But if we consider to how large a portion of the community it is of the first necessity that they should leave their homes in the morning physically fortified against the fatigues of an anxious day, it will at once be seen that it is at least of equal importance to provide a nourishing appetitive breakfast as a good dinner.

Mary Hooper, *Handbook for the Breakfast Table*, 1873

Breakfast in 1845

That change of manners which has introduced late dinners and superseded hot suppers has very much improved the modern breakfast. Besides the ordinary articles of eggs, broiled fish, pickled herrings, sardinias, finnan haddocks, collared eels, beef, mutton, and goat hams, reindeer and beef tongues, sausages, potted meats, cold pies of game, etc. etc., a few stimulative hot, dressed dishes are, by a sort of tacit prescription, set especially apart for the *dejeuner à la fourchette* [knife and fork meal] of the gourmand and the sportsman. Of this number are broiled kidneys, calf's and lamb's liver fried with fine herbs, mutton cutlets à la Venetienne, Oxford John (collops of mutton or venison) and many kinds of broiled and fried fish, and other piquant, and yet solid preparations.

Margaret Dods, *The Cook & Housewife's Manual*, 1870 edition

A Highlander's Choice

Sir Hector Mackenzie enjoyed his meals and was a good hand at breakfast, being especially fond of Smoked Salmon and Venison Collops, at which none alive could match Kate Archy. If a dish met him with pepper in it, which he detested, he would quietly give it up, saying, perhaps, "I wish pepper was a guinea an ounce", or, "The Lord sent us meat; we know where the cooks come from." On the sideboard there always stood before breakfast a bottle of whisky, smuggled of course, with plenty of camomile flowers, bitter orange-peel and juniper berries in it—"bitters" we called it—and of this he had a wee glass always before we sat down to breakfast as a fine stomachic.

Osgood Mackenzie, A *Hundred Years in the Highlands*, 1924

A Modern Highland Breakfast

The guests are wakened by the skirling of the pipes. The family piper walks round the house, playing the rouse "Hey, Johnnie Cope, are ye wauken yet?" Breakfast is set in the hall, where a fire of peat and logs is burning. Through the open window comes the smell of pine and heather. The air is like wine. A long day on the hill lies ahead.

Porridge and Cream

Grilled Trout Fried Bacon and Mushrooms

Finnan Haddie with Poached Egg

Potted Venison Potted Grouse

Smoked Mutton Ham

Baps Griddle Scones Oatcakes

Heather Honey Butter Marmalade

Toast, brown and white

Tea, Coffee Fresh Fruit

F. Marian McNeill, *The Book of Breakfasts*, 1932

The Angler

PISCATOR. My honest Scholar, it is now past five of the clock: we will fish till nine; and then go to breakfast. Go you to yonder sycamore tree and hide your bottle of drink under the hollow root of it; for about that time, and in that place, we will make a brave breakfast with a piece of powdered beef and a radish or two, that I have in my fish-bag: we shall, I warrant you, make a good, honest, wholesome hungry breakfast.

Izaac Walton, *The Compleat Angler*, 1653

Breakfast at Rosemount Grange

Breakfast at Rosemount Grange was conducted pretty much on the London Club principle, each guest having his separate *menage*—viz., two teapots, one containing the beverage, the other the hot water, a small glass basin of sugar, a ditto butter-boat and cream-ewer, together with a muffin or bun, and a rack of dry toast. A common coffee-pot occupied the centre of the round-table, flanked on the one side with a well-filled egg-stand, and on the other with a dish of beautiful moor-edge honey. On the side-table were hot meats and cold, with the well-made household bread. Hence each man on coming down, rang for his own supply without reference to any one else—a great convenience to fox-hunters, who like riding leisurely on instead of going full tilt to cover.

R. S. Surtees, *Mr Facey Romford's Hounds*, 1865

FOWL OR FISH QUENELLES

Soak a cupful of bread crumbs in cream. Mix half a cupful of pounded fish or fowl, mix well with the foregoing, and also an ounce of fresh butter. Mix a well-beaten egg. With this (the white and yolk beaten separately), add pepper and salt and convert the whole into a paste. Roll the quenelles into the shape of an egg and poach them in a stewpan of white stock for fourteen minutes. The same mixture is good put into a buttered mould.

M. L. Allen, *Savoury Dishes for Breakfast*, 1886

KEDGEREE

A breakfast cup full of rice boiled and strained, four eggs boiled hard. Chop all together with some cold boiled fish. Put a large lump of butter in the stewpan and make the mince very hot. Season it well with salt, pepper, and add a gill of thick cream. Any cold boiled fish will do for the Kedgeree, but turbot, cod, or salmon is the best.

RECIPE FOR GRILL

First grill chicken, game, or bones of lamb or mutton in a good quantity of fresh butter. Make following sauce: a small quantity of Worcester, a little mustard, and a small quantity of Bengal Club chutney. Put these ingredients into a saucepan, make them hot, and pour over the grill and butter. The grill to be turned over once or twice with a fork and served.

AN EXCELLENT RECIPE FOR DEVILLED CHICKEN OR GAME

Take about two ounces of butter, half a tablespoonful of mustard, a tablespoonful of flour, pepper and salt. Mix well together on a plate with a pallet knife, then add one large tablespoonful of Harvey Sauce and one of Lea & Perrin's Worcester Sauce. Mix well. Mask over your pieces of chicken or game. Then take each piece and dip it in egg and breadcrumb. *Butter it well*, and place it under a grill till golden brown. Serve with a few drops of demi-glaze over it.

Georgiana, Countess of Dudley, *The Dudley Book of Cookery & Household Recipes*, 1910

PULLED AND DEVILLED PHEASANT

Poach one or more pheasants, according to the quantity required. Remove all white meat from the breast and pull into small pieces, and mix with a good creamy white sauce. Take the pinions and the legs and devil them as follows:

Two ounces of butter warmed, one dessertspoonful of mustard (dry), one tablespoonful of flour, one tablespoonful of Harvey Sauce, one tablespoonful of Worcester Sauce, pepper and salt. Mix well and dip in egg and breadcrumbs. Pour over the joints and butter well and place under grill in a tin to brown.

Serve the pulled pheasant and the grill in separate dishes. This is excellent, either for breakfast or luncheon.

Georgiana, Countess of Dudley, *A Second Dudley Book of Cookery*, 1914

SAUCE FOR A DEVIL

Warm two ounces of butter in a stewpan, mix with it one teaspoonful of mustard, one of Harvey Sauce and one of Worcester, a little black pepper, Cayenne pepper, and salt. Prepare the broil and put it on a plate, pour the sauce over it and let it stand for five or six hours *before* broiling it on a clear slow fire. The ingredients given are only to show the proper proportion of each.

A pinch of curry powder improves this.

Minnie, Lady Hindlip's Cookery Book, 1925

SAUTÉED CHICKEN OR GROUSE LIVERS

Take six chicken or grouse livers and divide them in halves. See that they are very fresh and free from gall. Place in a stewpan a piece of fresh butter, a little onion chopped very fine. Let this fry for one minute, then add the livers and fry them quickly a nice light brown. Add a little meat essence, a little chopped parsley, pepper and salt, and serve very hot for breakfast. This dish must be served at once, otherwise the livers become hard, which spoils them. This dish is equally good as a savoury.

Georgiana, Countess of Dudley, *The Dudley Book of Cookery & Household Recipes*, 1910

DEER'S LIVER

Cut the deer's liver in slices, dip each piece in flour, dust with salt and pepper and fry in clear butter until it is a golden brown. If used for breakfast, lightly mask it with demi-glaze. If for lunch, serve with a good brown sauce poured over it, to which is added a squeeze of lemon juice and a little chopped parsley.

Some pieces of fried bacon can be served with the liver.

Georgiana, Countess of Dudley, *A Second Dudley Book of Cookery*, 1914

GRILLED KIDNEYS AND LEMON JUICE

Cut four kidneys nearly in halves, grill them on a well-greased gridiron. When done, put on each some chopped onion, parsley, butter, and lemon juice, pepper and salt.

Winchester Cutlets

Take any cold cooked meat, mince and pound it; add an equal quantity of breadcrumbs, one ounce of butter, pepper, salt, cayenne and a little ketchup. Make this into a stiff paste with a raw egg, and shape into small cutlets with a little flour; egg, breadcrumb, and fry in hot fat. Put a small piece of uncooked macaroni into the end of each to represent the bone.

Pheasant or Chicken Soufflé

Mince the meat by putting it through a sausage-machine twice. Take a cupful of breadcrumbs, half a pint of good strong stock, put into a stewpan and boil until it leaves the pan clean; then stir in the yolks of three eggs, pepper and salt, six finely chopped mushrooms, two finely chopped truffles, and a large spoonful of chopped parsley. Whip up the whites to a stiff froth, and when the mixture is cold stir them lightly into it. Line the mould with buttered paper before you put the mixture into it.

Pheasant Rissoles, Chicken or Lobster

(Half a pound) Mince the white meat of a pheasant, mix a few breadcrumbs, pepper and salt to taste, a few chopped herbs, half a teaspoonful of minced lemon peel and some chopped mushrooms or truffles; add a little milk, some white stock and then put all together in a saucepan and stir over a bright fire (a wooden spoon) for ten minutes. Then turn out into a plate; mix in one raw egg and leave it six hours to cool, when the mixture will be quite hard. Make into balls, egg and breadcrumb, and fry in boiling fat sufficient to cover the rissoles. Garnish with parsley. After taking the rissoles out of the frying pan, place them on kitchen paper to drain off all grease.

M. L. Allen, *Savoury Dishes for Breakfast*, 1886

————————— Game Toast —————————

Cold grouse, Cream, Pepper, Salt;
Hot buttered Toast

Toast a slice of bread and spread it with salt butter. Pound some cold grouse, put it into a pan with a little cream, heat it, and season rather lightly to taste. Spread this thickly on the toast, and cut into small squares. Little heaps of chopped hard-boiled eggs may be placed on the top of each. Serve very hot.

F. Marian McNeill, *The Book of Breakfasts*, 1932

Refreshment in the Field

I STILL have the hay box, complete with its padded compartments, from which I ate sausages and mash on a partridge shoot in 1938. I believe it is a dish that is hard to better.

Lunches for gun or rod give room for infinite variety, their style depending on circumstance and individual whim. The covert shooter can arrange the Land Rover to bring hot food to a predestined place, to be eaten in warmth and comfort. The stalker, the seeker of ptarmigan on the high tops, or the fisher of hill lochs, is constrained by the size and weight of pockets or haversack. There is room for argument among sportsmen and women as to what the rations should be. Let each state his or her preference.

THE GUN

The Luncheon Cart at Hall Barn

It started life as an Irish car, and has been developed into something very much better. It holds lunch and all accessories, has an ice well, two seats, two benches, each of which takes to pieces and packs into the car. When in use, the usual seats are the buffets, the boards on either side on which the feet ought to rest serve the purposes of tables, at which the benches enable the shooters to sit and eat in comfort.

Augustus Grimble, *Leaves from a Game Book*, 1898

A Discussion

"Ours was a lunch sent out to us from the kitchen. A shooting lunch proper should be more, and less, than that. It should be a lunch to be carried in the pocket; no dishes, no knives, no forks; just a packet as light and small as is compatible with a sufficiency of food."

"What must we forgo? What should we choose or substitute?"

"Sandwiches," reflected O, who has inspirations of the obvious. "But of what?"

"Not at all," contradicted P. "Slices. Of chicken, packed side by side with bread and butter. Far better. Or half a partridge."

"Why half?" asked S. "A whole partridge quartered; bread and butter salted—most important, because you either lose salt, or forget it, or it blows away in the wind. And a slice of cold plum pudding. And two apples."

Eric Parker, The Shooting Week-End Book, N.D.

Dingley Dell

"Weal pie," said Mr Weller, soliloquising, as he arranged the eatables on the grass . . . "Tongue; well, that's a wery good thing when it an't a woman's. Bread—knuckle o' ham, reg'lar picter—cold beef in slices, wery good. What's in them stone jars, young touch-and-go?"

"Beer in this one," replied the boy, taking from his shoulder a couple of large stone bottles, fastened together by a leathern strap—"cold punch in t'other."

"And a wery good notion of a lunch it is, take it altogether," said Mr Weller, surveying his arrangements of the repast with great satisfaction. "Now, gen'l'm'n, 'fall on,' as the English said to the French when they fixed bagginets."

It needed no second invitation to induce the party to yield full justice to the meal; and as little pressing did it require to induce Mr Weller, the long gamekeeper, and the two boys, to station themselves on the grass, at a little distance, and do good execution upon a decent proportion of the viands. An old oak afforded a pleasant shelter to the group, and a rich prospect of arable and meadow land, intersected with luxuriant hedges, and richly ornamented with wood, lay spread out before them.

"This is delightful—thoroughly delightful!" said Mr Pickwick, the skin of whose expressive countenance was rapidly peeling off, with exposure to the sun.

"So it is: so it is, old fellow," replied Mr Wardle, "Come; a glass of punch!"

"With great pleasure," said Mr Pickwick; the satisfaction of whose countenance, after drinking it, bore testimony to the sincerity of the reply.

"Good," said Mr Pickwick, smacking his lips, "Very good. I'll take another. Cool; very cool. Come, gentlemen," continued Mr Pickwick still retaining his hold upon the jar, "a toast. Our friends at Dingley Dell."

Charles Dickens, *The Pickwick Papers*, 1836

Grouse Shooting on Speyside—c. 1786

. . . We were near the mouth of Glen Ennoch, and then depositing our champaign, lime, shrub, porter, etc., in one of the large snow-drifts . . . we agreed to dine there. On my way up, the pointers had found some game, and I killed at two points an old moorcock and a ptarmigant, which I ordered to be well picked and prepared for dinner.

Our dinner, which was soon dressed, proved an excellent one; the chief dish consisted of two brace and a half of ptarmigants and a moorcock [red grouse], a quarter of a pound of butter, some slices of Yorkshire-smoked ham, and reindeer's tongue; with some sweet herbs, pepper, etc., prepared by the housekeeper at Raits. These with a due proportion of water, made each of us a plate of very strong soup . . .

Thomas Thornton, A *Sporting Tour*, 1804

IRISH STEW AND PLUM PUDDING

My own earliest recollection of shooting lunches is of a great iron pot that, swathed in heat-containing blankets, came out in a farm-cart. This great pipkin held a piping hot Irish stew of the obsolete sort that is never forgotten. Heavens, how good it was!—the potatoes (those atop plentifully dusted with coarse black pepper), the pale, the delicate, portions of smoking young rabbit, the streaky boiled bacon, the occasional plump pigeon, the pink and tender cutlet, and, embracing the perfect whole, what consistent succulence of simmering stock! Ah, me! And then, after a greasy quarter of an hour, came cold slices of dark plum-pudding, nestling in layers of white sugar and/or a wedge of Scotch bun, made as it *could* only be made in Angus.

Patrick Chalmers, The Shooting Man's England, c. 1930

————————— Hot Curry or Collops —————————

Let me give you a cold-day tip for an outdoor dish. We will presume that luncheon is to be sent out for six guns. Get, therefore, six white earthenware jam pots of the usual nursery size. Fill two-thirds of each with a sizzling hot curry and top up with equally hot boiled rice. Cover with parchment paper, secure the same with string or elastic bands, and pack all six contiguously with a towel or fair napkin over all. They will keep piping hot for an hour; they occupy no space; and the hot pots warm the hands of the luncher even as their contents warm his heart. And a spoon will serve him.

If hot collops be preferred to curry, then substitute a crown of mashed potato for the rice. And note that with the both of them chutney goes nicely.

Patrick R. Chalmers, At The Sign of The Dog & Gun, 1930

Cold Grouse

Nothing is better for a spartan lunch by the spring on the hillside than half a cold grouse with oat-cake, and a beaker or two of whisky and water.

Alexander Innes Shand, Shooting, 1902

Indoors

I think that to lunch indoors asks little art of menu. The ordinary serves—cold meats and hot potatoes, a new-made currant cake, cheese and a stick or so of sounding celery, and to drink, strong old ale poured from tall jugs of crystal, with weak whisky and soda a bad second. Wine, so very admirable after sunset, is, other than a culminating glass of light port, an indecency at luncheon.

Patrick Chalmers, *The Shooting Man's England*, c. 1930

MRS TURNER'S INDOOR SHOOTING LUNCH

For Partridge Pudding, take two brace of old partridges and cut them into neat joints, season with two teaspoonfuls of salt and a teaspoonful of pepper, some chopped parsley and herbs, and add a few mushrooms if you have them. Line a greased pudding basin holding two quarts with a thick suet crust, and lay a thin slice of rump steak weighing about a quarter pound at the bottom, then a layer of partridges and seasoning up to the top; place another slice of rump steak rather larger but quite thin over this. Have ready about two pints of good stock (flavouring it with two glasses of claret is an improvement but not essential), and pour this over your partridges in the basin. Cover carefully with your suet crust and pinch the edges together. Tie a pudding cloth over the basin, place in boiling water and keep boiling for quite three hours till ready. This pudding is big enough for eight guns.

Eric Parker, *The Shooting Week-End Book*, N.D.

Beaters' Lunch

When beaters lunch within, their likes, which we must study, vary with locality. With us, here in Oxfordshire, cold Red Elephant is a hot favourite. Red Elephant? Bless me, don't you know? Red Elephant's our local love-name for boiled silverside.

Patrick Chalmers, *The Shooting Man's England*, c. 1930

Tommiebeg

Oh! the pleasure of that mid-day halt on the moor! Like the rich patch of verdure in the midst of the brown heather, it is an oasis in life, surpassing delicious in the present and a bright spot to look back at in the future. To Captain Downey, again all this was a matter of course—it was part of the day's work;—not that even he, the case-hardened, was not alive to the gratification of restoring the inner man by creature comforts, and refreshing the weary limbs for the fatigues yet before him; but to Brixey, it was something more. It was perfect happiness.

It was some time, however, before he could go to work at the substantial part of the entertainment. Sandy was instrumental in bringing him "to this complexion". First he poured over his hands some cold fresh water from the spring, then he administered a judicious portion of Glenlivet, mixed with a smaller proportion of the pure element,—and Brixey, rightly considering that the natives of the country must necessarily be well acquainted with the requirements of the climate, took, without demurring, another quantum of "the mixture as before", when it was presented to him. By these simple remedies he was soon in a condition to fall to with great zest, at the cold grouse and sundry other good things, which he washed down with a horn or two of capital Scotch ale, nearly iced, from having been sometime bathing in the cool spring,—and then he followed the Captain's example, and lighted a cigar. He could not find the heart to refuse, under these circumstances, another horn of ale which Sandy poured out for him; and as another bottle was open, and Downey declined it, he helped Sandy and Archie to dispose of it.

Thomas Jeans, *The Tommiebeg Shootings*, c. 1860

Pies in Blankets

In Yorkshire, when driving grouse late in the season on a well-known moor, we had for lunch most delicious pies made with grouse, rabbits, and potatoes, and although they had to be brought some six or seven miles from the lodge, they were as hot as if they had just come out of the oven, having been carried in a clothes basket wrapped up in blankets. The blankets must be new ones!

The Proper Thing

A relation of mine with whom I shoot a great deal, does what I consider the proper thing. At lunch time, if the weather is fine, one of Edgington's paragon tables, which rolls up into a very small compass, with seats to match, is laid out, in a sheltered spot, when we regale ourselves with good cold joints, baked potatoes, cake, biscuits and cheese accompanied by either beer, or whisky and soda, with a "tot up" of good old brown sherry. The beaters are supplied with plenty of cold meat, bread, and slices of cold plum pudding, washed down with a copious supply of beer, and then an ounce of baccy to each man. Needless to say, they all start again thoroughly refreshed and happy with themselves and their master.

It is a shame to see the way beaters, who have all the hard work to do, are treated in some places—very often they have nothing more satisfying to work on than a piece of stale bread and a hunk of rank cheese.

The Dangers of Peat Water

. . . that moss water that lies amongst the peat-bogs . . . Mac-Collie the Keeper tells me that it's so full of vegetation that without a little whisky to kill it, a young tree might take root in my inside, and that he kenned a man who died, and that the oak-tree is growing straight up out of the centre of his grave yet.

Women Unwelcome

Ladies are very fond of putting in an appearance at a shooting lunch; this is all very well if they go home with the empty dishes, but when you are addressed as follows in a pleading tone: "Oh! Mr So-and-So, do you mind me standing beside you while you shoot?" What are you to do unless you are downright rude and refuse point blank; your sport is spoilt for the afternoon if you are one of the guns posted forward, in covert shooting especially. Ladies will not and cannot keep quiet, they get excited and make the birds break back. I cannot vote for woman suffrage in the shooting field.

Fores's Sporting Notes and Sketches, 1898

THE RIFLE

The Flask

Go early into the field, take with you some rum in a wicker bottle that will hold about a gill; this will keep out or expel wind, cure the gripes, and give spirits when fatigued; but do not take too much, for too much will make your sight unsteady.

Thomas Fairfax, *The Complete Sportsman*, N.D.

Drinking—An Admonition

Do not drink any water for the first three days, and you will require very little for the rest of the season. If, on a hot day, you drink at every spring, by two o'clock you will feel like a water-butt only fit to roll down hill. If very hot and thirsty, turn up your sleeves and immerse your arms up to the elbows in water. It cools the blood, and doing so quenches the thirst.

Lord Walsingham & Sir Ralph Payne-Gallwey, *Shooting: Moor & Marsh*, 1887

Another Admonition

. . . I will not limit him, as Sir Humphrey does his fisherman, to the philosopher's half pint of claret; but if he exceed it, 'tis at his own peril. Wine and poetry go joyously together. Bacchus and Apollo were aye boon companions; but I never heard of Diana having attached herself to the jolly god, or of an amour between Hebe and Adonis. Hard work upon wine will parch up the body, and make the hand rickety . . . During the first week your mouth will be drinking bog water in every black pool you can find; in the next your flesh will vanish from your solitary bones; and in the third,—yes, in the third, at latest, you will die by spontaneous combustion.

William Scrope, *The Art of Deer Stalking*, 1839

―――――――――――― Mr Chaytor's Mull ――――――――――――

And if you are very wet and cold and hot drink you *must* have, here is Mr Chaytor's recipe for the most Olympian mull that ever man brewed. Take a shred of lemon rind, three cloves, and two egg-cupfuls of water and simmer together for a few minutes. Then add a pint of claret and warm till nearly boiling. Add five lumps of sugar and a wine-glass of cherry brandy and serve in a small jug with claret glasses.

Patrick Chalmers, *The Shooting Man's England*, c. 1930

The Stalker's Choice

The reveille sounded at 7.30; breakfast followed at 8.30, during which meal we gave a name to what each preferred put up for his lunch, and, though there was always a choice to be made from a variety of good things, there was extraordinary unanimity shown in voting day by day for egg sandwiches with a few ginger nuts or a piece of shortbread with some fruit.

Augustus Grimble, *More Leaves from My Game Book*, 1917

Lunch for the Pocket

Should a deer-stalker eat and stuff? Should he pamper the inward man? Shade of Abernethy forbid! . . . to restrict him entirely from the venison pasty, would be a cruelty from which our indulgent nature is averse; we wish to be liberal in these matters . . . He may dilute with tea and possess himself of a few grapes to cool him. Peaches and nectarines may be put in his pocket, because, as he will be sure to sit upon them, they will do him no earthly harm, but rather confer a benefit by moistening the outward man . . . But here I must stop . . . for would you have me fill my man with Finnon Haddocks and all the trashy and unprofitable varieties of marmalade: red, green, and orange?

William Scrope, *The Art of Deer Stalking*, 1839

BOOKMAKER SANDWICHES

In his book, *La Cuisine Anglaise*, M. Suzanne gives the following kind of sandwich, which deserves attention:

This kind of sandwich, which is liked by racing people, is a most substantial affair, and it will be seen from the following recipe that a sandwich of the nature prescribed might, in an emergency, answer the purpose of a meal.

Take an English tin-loaf, and cut off its two end crusts, leaving on them about one-third inch of crumb. Butter these crusts. Meanwhile grill a thick steak, well seasoned with salt and pepper. When it is cooked, cool it; sprinkle it with grated horse-radish and mustard, and lay it between the two crusts. String the whole together as for a galantine, and wrap it in several sheets of blotting-paper. Then place the parcel under a letter-press, the screw of which should be gradually tightened, and leave the sandwich thus for one half hour.

At the end of this time the insides of the slices of bread have, owing to the pressure, become saturated with meat juice, which is prevented from escaping by the covering of crust.

Remove the blotting-paper, and pack the sandwich in a box or in several sheets of white paper.

A. Escoffier, A Guide to Modern Cookery, 1926

A Lady Stalker's Abstinence

. . . my "piece" usually is forgotten, or not required, till near four o'clock. What does one want with food till then after a good breakfast at half-past eight or nine o'clock, when one is out and up in the finest air in the world? That is the food for the hill, more wholesome and easily digested than any other.

Hilda Murray, Echoes of Sport, 1910

Whisky or Port?

Whisky is most usually carried, but the writer has found nothing so well suited for a long day as a flask holding three or four glasses of good old port wine. The warmth and fillip it gives is much more lasting than whisky, and at lunch save a biscuit and a glass for five o'clock tea.

Augustus Grimble, Deer-Stalking, 1888

Tea

. . . tea—the best drink a tired man can have (if I have any hard walking to do, as in deer-stalking, I always carry cold tea, without sugar or cream, in my flask, instead of anything stronger) . . .

James Conway, Forays among Salmon & Deer, 1861

Home from the Hill

The best part of a bottle of champagne may be allowed at dinner: this is not only venial, but salutary. A few tumblers of brandy and soda-water are greatly to be commended, for they are cooling. Whisky cannot reasonably be objected to, for it is an absolute necessary, and does not come under the name of intemperance, but rather, as Dogberry says, or ought to say, "it comes by nature". Ginger-beer I hold to be a dropsical, insufficient, and unmanly beverage; I pray you avoid it; and as for your magnums and pottle-deep potations, as Captain Bobadil says, "We cannot extend thus far."

William Scrope, *The Art of Deer Stalking*, 1839

Persia

On one occasion I was invited by a Persian Minister to take part in a drive of ibex and moufflon from the higher ground into the valleys. Large numbers of does passed the rifles, at which a brisk fusillade was kept up by the Persians without much result. But what impressed this expedition on my memory was the Persian luncheon in the open in which I had to take part. The food was excellent, poached eggs and roast lamb cooked on the spot. There were no plates nor knives and forks, and until I had seen my hosts do it I was much perturbed how to eat a poached egg with my fingers, but with skill it can be done without breaking the surface of the egg. As the honoured guest my hosts tore off pieces of lamb with their fingers and handed them to me, but happily I had noticed that they had all washed their hands before sitting down to the meal. It was an interesting experience.

Lord Hardinge of Penshurst, *On Hill and Plain*, 1933

THE ROD

Sub Jove

When fishing by oneself, so that the ration has to be carried on the person, a cold chop, or a chicken leg that can be held by the bone, with a bread and cheese sandwich fills the bill. The trout you have

been waiting for all the morning always rises just as you unpack
your lunch, so that it is well to have something that you can hold
in one hand while playing your art with the other.

Sir Francis Colchester-Wemyss, The Pleasures of the Table, 1931

An Angler's Excursion

I resolved to start early next morning for my favourite river, the
Dartion; it was distant about fourteen miles . . . and if sport was
good I often remained overnight in a cave close to the river,
consequently some preparation was necessary. On this occasion I
first of all superintended the packing of a "learthern conve-
niency", made for the purpose, with "grub" for the excursion (and
allow me to advise you, if you ever should require it, personally to
superintend this most necessary preparation for a night in a cave;
and don't trust to either wife or servant, for, in their anxiety to do
good, they give what one does not want, and sometimes leave out
what one does). That you may know what is good to take, I shall
tell you what I packed up. A venison ham (salt meat is no
objection by a river side), a heap of oat cakes, a few hard biscuits, a
homemade cheese, some tea, sugar, salt, etc.; a knife and fork,
and a small tin kettle, which answered as teapot as well; and, of
course, a bottle of whisky.

James Conway, Forays among Salmon & Deer, 1861

Trout and Barley Wine

. . . my friend is an honest countryman, and his name is Coridon;
and he is a downright witty companion, that met me here
purposely to be pleasant and eat a Trout . . . Come, hostess, dress
it presently; and get us what other meat the house will afford; and
give us some of your best barley-wine, the good liquor that our
honest forefathers did use to think of; the drink which preserved
their health, and made them live so long, and to do so many good
deeds.

A Wet Day

. . . And Coridon and I have not had an unpleasant day: and yet I have caught but five trouts; for, indeed, we went to a good honest ale-house, and there we played at shovel-board half the day; all the time that it rained we were there, and as merry as they that fished. And I am glad we are now with a dry house over our heads; for hark! how it rains and blows. Come, hostess, give us more ale, and our supper with what haste you may . . . and therefore let's go merrily to supper, and then have a gentle touch at singing and drinking; but the last with moderation.

Angler's Punch

And pray let's now rest ourselves in the sweet shady arbour, which nature herself has woven with her own fine fingers; 'tis such a contexture of woodbines, sweetbriar, jasmine, and myrtle; and so interwoven, as will secure us both from the sun's violent heat and from the approaching shower. And being set down, I will requite a part of your courtesies with a bottle of sack, milk, oranges, and sugar, which, all put together, make a drink like nectar; indeed, too good for any but us Anglers.

Izaac Walton, *The Compleat Angler*, 1653

MULLED CLARET

My Dear Boys,—There are a few miscellaneous hints that I should like to give you, though most of them are not connected with salmon fishing.

The first one, however, is, or was so, for on cold days on getting home from the river we used always to find ready for us in the fender a jug of the most excellent brew that I have ever tasted—a hot mulled claret, and this is Falshaw's receipt for it:

Take a shred of lemon rind, three cloves, and two egg-cupfuls of water, and simmer these together for a few minutes. Then add a pint of claret and warm until it is nearly boiling. Add four to five lumps of sugar and, if you wish, two to three teaspoonfuls of cherry brandy, and serve in a small jug with claret glasses.

A. H. Chaytor, *Letters to a Salmon Fisher's Sons*, 1910

Game Pie

HE, or she, who invented the game pie deserves the gratitude of mankind. Those who seek something good and substantial to eat on a picnic, or on a journey, need look no further. A cold pie tucked in the suitcase on a train will allay apprehension of late arrival and of a wearisome night-time search for somewhere decent to eat at the other end. Above all, I recommend it when you are a house guest. Your hostess will certainly ask you again.

Of proprietary pies Fortnum & Mason's are the most celebrated. I once knew a Territorial Army soldier who, when on weekend exercises on Salisbury Plain, would have a game pie delivered to him from Fortnum's. What a gloriously incongruous sight the delivery van must have been in the midst of mock battle.

In terms of economy the game pie is the virtuous means of using up old birds, and any game that is badly shot and therefore unsuitable for roasting.

ANGEL'S PIE

Many people would call this a pigeon pie, for in good sooth there be pigeons in it; but 'tis a pie worthy of a brighter sphere than this.

Six plump young pigeons, trimmed of all superfluous matter, including pinions and below the thighs. Season with pepper and salt, and stuff these pigeons with foie gras, and quartered truffles, and fill up the pie with plovers' eggs and some good force-meat. Make a good gravy from the superfluous parts of the birds, and some calf's head stock to which has been added about half a wine-glassful of old Madeira, with some lemon-juice and cayenne. See that your paste be light and flaky, and bake in a moderate oven for three hours. Pour in more gravy just before taking out, and let the pie get cold.

This is a concoction which will make you back all the winners; whilst no heiress who nibbles at it would refuse you her hand and heart afterwards.

Edward Spencer, *Cakes & Ale*, 1897

Périgord Pie

Clean and bone four grouse or six partridges, divide each bird into four, and sprinkle with aromatic spices, pepper, and salt. Put on the bones and giblets, in a stew-pan with white stock, let them simmer for two hours, then strain into a basin, and, if necessary, season with a little pepper and Ketchup. Line the pie-dish with very thin slices of Wiltshire bacon, inside of which put another lining of nicely seasoned veal and ham, forcemeat, with as many sliced truffles and mushrooms (chiefly truffles) as possible stuck into it; now put in the half of the game in a layer, filling up the spaces with forcemeat, truffles, and mushrooms, then the other half of the game cover all over with forcemeat and then with thin slices of bacon. Make a sufficient quantity of flour and water paste, with which cover the pie, making one or two holes in it for the escape of the steam, and bake in a moderate oven for three hours. When ready, take it out of the oven, remove the paste, and pour the previously prepared stock, which should be boiling, over it, let it stand till cold and set, then cover with clarified butter, and put aside for use. When wanted remove the cake of butter, cover with aspic jelly, arranged in stripes of rose and amber, with a wreath of parsley round the border of the dish. The dish itself, being perfectly plain, may be ornamented with bands of gold or silver paper, or a wreath of evergreens, or anything the occasion or taste may suggest. Fireproof stoneware dishes, rather deep and quite plain, are used for this pie, and may be had at any good china shop. Game of any sort may be used instead of what has been named in the recipe, or, when it is quite out of season, pigeons or poultry may be substituted, but the truffles cannot be omitted, as it is owing to the quantity used in the making of this dish, that it is called Périgord Pie.

D. Williamson, *The Practice of Cookery & Pastry . . .* , 1884

A Cold Raised Game Pie

To make the paste, take one pound of flour, four ounces of butter, a teaspoonful of salt, one gill and a half of hot water. Place the flour on your slab, make a hollow in the centre. Put the butter, water and salt into a stewpan over the fire until it is heated, but not hotter than your hand could bear. Pour this gradually into the flour, and mix it quickly with your hand, taking care to knead the whole firmly into a compact paste, roll in a napkin and keep it in a warm place until ready for use. With this paste you line your raised pie mould, which has been well greased. Place it on a baking sheet with two thicknesses of foolscap paper round the outside of the mould. When the mould is lined with paste, you next line again with slices of fat bacon cut very thin. At the bottom of the mould place some forcemeat made with veal and fat bacon in equal proportions, some foie gras, slices of truffles, some fillets of hare (or venison) well seasoned, pheasant, partridge, or any game freed from bone or sinew, repeat the foie gras, then again the forcemeat until the pie is full, putting in a very little good essence, sufficient to moisten the meat. Cover the top with the paste, ornamenting it with fancy leaves cut in the paste with a cutter, leaving a hole in the centre to let out the steam. Wash over with egg and bake for about four hours, steadily, then set on one side to cool. Have ready about one pint of strong game consommé well seasoned, pour this into the pie by the aid of a small funnel through the hole in the centre. Take the pie out of the mould, and serve cold on a side table.

Georgiana, Countess of Dudley, *The Dudley Book of Cookery & Household Recipes*, 1910

Venison Pie

Cut some pieces of venison, either from the neck or loin or part of a haunch. Add pepper and salt, two finely chopped onions and a little parsley, two or three hard-boiled eggs cut in quarters, a little chopped mushroom and two sheeps' kidneys cut into small pieces.

Place this in layers in a deep pie dish, and cover with plenty of good stock or gravy.

Make a good half puff pastry with three-quarters of a pound of flour and a pound of butter or lard, rolling it as for puff pastry. Cover the pie with this and egg over. Bake for an hour and a half.

------------------------------ HARE PIE ------------------------------

One small hare, half a pound of calf's liver, four ounces of bacon, one shallot, half a clove of garlic, two ounces of butter, seasoning, herbs, thyme, marjoram (half a teaspoonful of each), one glass of port wine, one egg, a spoonful of red currant jelly, a little stock and a suitable paste crust. Skin the hare and wash it several times in fresh water; cut into joints and bone each. Put the carcass in a stewpan with water, to make stock; flavour with cloves, a little sauce, bay leaf and salt. Skim as it boils, and cook gently for one hour. Wipe the meat; cut it into slices and fry in an ounce of butter; add the shallot, peeled and chopped; take out the meat and let cool. Add the remainder of butter to the stewpan in which the hare was fried; when hot put in the calf's liver, previously sliced thinly, and two ounces of the bacon; fry for a short time and pound all in a mortar till smooth. Rub this through a wire sieve and mix with a well-beaten egg. Season with salt, pepper, and aromatic season-ing. Line a raised pie-mould with hot water; prick the bottom and sides with a fork; line the sides and bottom with thin slices of bacon and with a layer of the prepared farce; fill up the mould with the fried pieces of hare. Sprinkle the powdered herbs and seasoning in between; moisten each layer with port wine and red currant jelly; cover the top with farce and lay on the crust; fix the latter firmly. Decorate with pieces of paste. Make a suitable incision in the centre of the cover of crust, to allow the steam to escape whilst cooking. Bake in a moderate oven from one and a half to two and a quarter hours, according to the size of the pie. As the pie leaves the oven pour a little well-reduced stock into it; this is best done by means of a funnel.

    This pie can be served either hot or cold.

Georgiana, Countess of Dudley, A Second Dudley Book of Cookery, 1914

------------------------------ RABBIT PIE ------------------------------

. . . much of the excellence depends on a judicious use of adjuncts. Mushrooms are almost indispensable, and even the freshest truffles are not wasted. Slices of egg are a decided improvement, and some people advocate forcemeat balls, though that is more open to question. At any rate, there can be no doubt about eschalots, anchovies, or Norwegian sprats, with butter or shred suet. But, above all, the pie should be paved with slices of fat bacon, and bacon should be interpolated through the pieces of rabbit. Strain the gravy, which should be boiled to a jelly. Crown with a rich puff-paste, and bake the pie according to size.

A. I. Shand, *The Cookery of Rabbit*, 1898

GROUSE PIE

The simplest form of grouse pie merely requires the birds (jointed, halved, or sometimes whole), a proportion (a pound to a brace is usual) of rump steak cut into knobs, seasoning, crust, and a sufficiency of good gravy (which may or may not be touched up with lemon juice and claret) to fill up and moisten the mixture. To this, of course, the usual enrichments of hard eggs . . . mushrooms, truffles, forcemeat balls, and so forth, may be added. These additions merge themselves very much in the general "game pie", an excellent thing in its way no doubt. But I do not know that it is so good as the simple grouse pie with nothing added but steak, seasoning, an alliaceous touch of some sort, and a few eggs and mushrooms.

George Saintsbury, *The Cookery of the Grouse*, 1895

PARTRIDGE PIE

Two young partridges, three-quarters of a pound of lean veal, half a pound of boiled bacon or gammon, one gill of Soubise or onion sauce, one ounce of butter, two hard-boiled eggs, chopped parsley, preserved or fresh mushrooms, salt, pepper, and aromatic seasoning. Puff or rough paste for covering.

Truss the birds; divide them into halves and fry them slightly in a sauté pan with the butter. Line a pie dish with thin slices of lean veal and bacon; lay in the birds; season with chopped mushrooms, chopped parsley, salt, pepper and a good pinch of aromatic spice. Put a layer of veal and bacon slices on the top, and pour the sauce over this; cover this with the slices of hard-boiled eggs. Roll out the paste, and cover the pie in the usual manner. Bake for a full hour in a fairly well-heated oven, and pour a little rich stock or gravy into the pie as it leaves the oven. Serve either hot or cold.

Georgiana, Countess of Dudley, *A Second Dudley Book of Cookery*, 1914

Rook Pie

Young rooks, by being first skinned, and then soaked all night in cold spring water, make pies, which are worthy the notice of the most scientific gourmand.

Lt-Col. P. Hawker, *Instructions to Young Sportsmen*, 1814

WOODCOOK PIE

This wonderful dish varies slightly in construction, some authorities holding that it should be made of a blanket of well-beaten fillet steak on which a brace of woodcock are placed breast downward; then the interslices are packed with chopped bacon, onion rings, and seasoning, the whole then covered by another steak, and finally the pie-crust. This is, I fancy, the real British recipe.

The second school is more probably French. The pie-dish is lined with bacon, then a layer of calves' liver in slices; on this are laid joints of woodcock, and the trail (insides), mixed with ham and bacon forcemeat, is poured over them and the whole is capped with pie-crust and served with a white wine and truffle sauce. This last appears to be pure epicurean extravagance.

PIGEON PIE I

Either halved or jointed pigeons and thin slices of rump steak and hard-boiled eggs arranged in layers in good stock in a pie-dish covered with pie-crust.

H. B. C. Pollard, *The Sportsman's Cookery Book*, 1926

PIGEON PIE II

Lay a border of fine puff paste round a large dish, and cover the bottom with a veal cutlet or tender rump steak, free from fat and bone and seasoned with salt, cayenne and nutmeg or pounded mace; prepare with great nicety as many freshly killed young pigeons as the dish will contain in one layer; put into each a slice or ball of butter, seasoned with a little cayenne and mace, lay them into the dish with the breasts downwards, and between and over them put the yolks of half a dozen or more of hard-boiled eggs; stick plenty of butter on them, season the whole well with salt and spice, pour in some cold water or veal broth for the gravy, roll out the cover three-quarters of an inch thick, secure it well round the edge, ornament it highly, and bake the pie for an hour or more in a well-heated oven. It is a great improvement to fill the birds with small mushroom-buttons, prepared as for partridges [see recipe on page 132]. Their livers also may be put into them.

Eliza Acton, *Modern Cookery for Private Families*, 1845

Pigeon Pie III

Which is best served hot, and is more suited to the dining-room than the race-course.

Line a pie dish with veal force-meat, very highly seasoned, about an inch thick. Place on it some thin slices of fat bacon, three pigeons (trimmed) in halves, a veal sweetbread in slices, an ox palate, boiled and cut up into dice, a dozen asparagus tops, a few button mushrooms (the large ones would give the interior of the pie a bad colour) and the yolks of four eggs. Cover with force-meat and bake for three hours. Some good veal gravy should be served with this.

Goose Pie

Here is a quaint old eighteenth century recipe, which comes from Northumberland, and is given verbatim.

Bone a goose, a turkey, a hare, and a brace of grouse; skin it, and cut off all the outside pieces—I mean of the tongue, after boiling it—lay the goose, for the outside a few pieces of hare; then lay in the turkey, the grouse, and the remainder of the tongue and hare. Season highly between each layer with pepper and salt, mace and cayenne, and put it together, and draw it close with a needle and thread. Take 20 lbs of flour, put 5 lbs of butter into a pan with some water, let it boil, pour it among the flour, stir it with a knife, then work it with your hands till quite stiff. Let it stand before the fire for half an hour, then raise your pie and set it to cool; then finish it, put in the meat, close the pie, and set it in a cold place. Ornament according to your taste, bandage it with calico dipped in fat. Let it stand all night before baking. It will take a long time to bake. The oven must be pretty hot for the first four hours, and then allowed to slacken. To know when it is enough, raise one of the ornaments, and with a fork try if the meat is tender. If it is hard the pie must be put in again for two hours more. After it comes out of the oven fill up with strong stock, well seasoned, or with clarified butter.

Verily, in the eighteenth century they must have had considerably more surplus cash and time, and rather more angelic cooks than their descendants.

Edward Spencer, *Cakes & Ale*, 1897

PUDDING

Cut four pigeons each into four pieces, discarding the back-bones. Dice 6 oz ham and 6 oz beefsteak and mix with the pieces of pigeon, adding a teaspoonful of chopped parsley, half teaspoonful chopped thyme, 2 oz sliced mushrooms and a good sprinkling of salt and pepper.

Line a basin with good suet crust, and fill with the meat mixture and quarter pint good clear stock. Cover with a lid of suet crust, making sure to pinch it well at the edges to form a perfect seal.

Do not boil the pudding, but steam it for two and a half hours.

PLOVER PIE

Line a pie-dish with slices of ham and cover the bottom with peeled mushrooms. Split as many plover as will fill the dish, filling up the gaps here and there with more peeled mushrooms and slices of hard-cooked egg. Sprinkle with pepper, but be careful with the salt because of the ham content; top up with thin brown gravy to within half inch of the top of the pie-dish.

Cover with puff-pastry, brush well over with beaten egg, and bake at 450 degrees F for the first 15 minutes, and then at 375 degrees F for 45 minutes. Take up the pie, add more hot gravy if desired, and serve.

Henry Smith, *The Master Book of Poultry & Game*, c. 1950

──────────────────── SALMON PIE ────────────────────

Take slices of raw salmon half an inch thick. Put coarse black pepper
between them and a pinch of salt. Cover with pie crust—bake and eat
cold.

Georgiana, Countess of Dudley, *The Dudley Book of Cookery & Household Recipes*, 1910

──────────────── CORNISH MIXED FISH PIE ────────────────

Toss the fish in seasoned flour, and lay them in a well-buttered pie-dish.
Add some chopped parsley and a minced onion. Cover with meat broth
and put on a pastry lid with a hole in the centre.

When baked, pour in a little cream through the hole, and serve at
once.

──────────────── SALMON AND SHRIMP PIE ────────────────

Butter the bottom and sides of a pie dish and line it with puff pastry. Cut
up the salmon in cutlets and lay them in the dish; season with cayenne,
common pepper and salt, add some bruised shrimps and fill the pie
about half-full of water. Put on the lid of the pastry, gild it with egg
yolk, make a hole in the top and bake for thirty minutes with the
Regulo at Mark 7. Meanwhile, with the salmon bones, head and any
other ingredients you have at hand, make a good gravy and when the
pie is done pour this through the hole in the top. Serve hot.

Margaret Butterworth, *Now Cook Me The Fish*, 1950

──────────────── KOULIBIAK (RUSSIAN) ────────────────

Ingredients. 2 lbs of "choux" paste (Puff pastry is a simple alternative),
2 lbs of salmon, cut in small steaks, ½ lb of Kascha or rice, a few dried
mushrooms, 1 onion, a sprig of fennel, salt, pepper.

Method. Roll the paste out on a floured board and divide in two
rectangular sheets of equal size. On one sheet of pastry put a layer of the
cooked Kascha or rice, mixed with the chopped onion and chopped
mushrooms, *also* previously cooked. Then lay the slices of cooked
salmon on this, and cover with another layer of Kascha. Over this put

the other sheet of paste, damping the edges slightly and pressing firmly. Make a slight opening in the centre of the Koulibiak, so that the steam can escape, brush over with melted butter, and put in a moderate oven for about 45 minutes, till the paste is of a golden colour.

Countess Morphy, *Recipes of All Nations*, c. 1930

EEL PIE

1 medium sized eel
2 cups good stock
Salt & Pepper
Pinch mixed herbs

1 onion
Lemon juice to taste
Good light Piecrust

The eel should be cut into pieces, after skinning, and placed in a pan with the fins, head and tail portion. Add the stock, salt, pepper, herbs and sliced onion. Cook gently until the fish is just done enough to enable one to remove centre bone. Strain liquid, skimming well. Place the pieces of eel in a pie-dish, season with lemon juice, add stock, cover with pastry and bake in a rather hot oven for about one hour. The stock may, if desired, be slightly thickened by the addition of a tablespoonful of flour mixed with half the stock, the remainder being added—warm—to the pie as soon as taken from the oven, pouring it in through a funnel under the central rose decoration.

André L. Simon, *Fish*, 1940

Jellies and Dressings

PROVIDENCE has so ordered things that the fruits of the countryside are perfect accompaniments to the game birds and beasts that habitually feed on them.

We claim no exotica at Cromlix, but common wild produce lends itself well to our dishes. Elderflowers are earliest. Boiled and strained, there is no more refreshing flavouring for sorbet. Later, elderberries make a useful addition to jellies of other fruits such as blackberry, or added to apple pies. One day I shall make elderberry ketchup, also known as Pontack sauce, the title derived from a Victorian restaurant of that name in London. One never hears of it now, but it was a favourite with game.

Red currants come in July, as do wild raspberries towards the end of the month. The small berries have an intensity of flavour unmatched by domestic varieties. At the same time the blaeberries, or blueberries, ripen on the moor among the heather stems, and grouse gather eagerly to feed on them. We have never picked them, because to gather a good quantity would take hours scouring through dense heather. Nursery catalogues are now offering plants for sale, so perhaps we will try them in the fruit garden.

The rowan trees provide the last of the berries, ripening in late September or early October. It takes judgement to pick them fully ripe, and the birds are waiting for that moment too. You may arrive a day or two late, and the trees are bare. Rowan jelly's sharp taste is a perfect foil to the richness of game.

Rules for Seasoning

As a general rule, bachelors and sportsmen to be allowed a fourth more seasoning than sober married men.

Margaret Dods, *The Cook & Housewife's Manual*, 1870 edition

His Mother's Storeroom

. . . where could a storeroom be seen like my mother's at Conon? The room was shelved all round with movable frames for holding planks, on which unimaginable quantities of dried preserved edibles reposed till called for. There were jam-pots by the hundred of every sort, shelves of preserved candied apricots and Magnum Bonum plums, that could not be surpassed in the world; other shelves with any amount of biscuits of all sorts of materials, once liquid enough to drop on sheets of paper, but in time dried to about two inches across and half an inch thick for dessert. Smoked sheep and deer tongues were also there, and from the roof hung strings of threaded artichoke bottoms, dried, I suppose, for putting into soups. In addition, there were endless curiosities of confectionery brought north by Kitty's talents from her Edinburgh cookery school, while quantities of dried fruit, ginger, orange-peel, citron, etc. from North Simpson & Graham of London must have made my dear mother safe—cased in armour against any unexpected and hungry invader. Then every year she made gooseberry and currant wines, balm ditto, raspberry vinegar, spruce and ginger beer. I remember they were celebrated, and liqueurs numberless included magnums of camomile flowers and orange-peel and gentian root bitters for old women with indigestion pains.

Osgood Mackenzie, *A Hundred Years in the Highlands*, 1924

—————— RASPBERRY VINEGAR ——————

Put a pound of very fine raspberries in a bowl, bruise them well, and pour upon them a quart of the best white wine vinegar. Next day strain the liquor on a pound of fresh ripe raspberries; bruise them also, and on the following day do the same, but do not squeeze the fruit, or it will make it ferment, only drain the liquor as dry as you can from it. Finally, pass it through a canvas bag previously wet with the vinegar to prevent waste. Put the juice into a stone jar with a pound of sugar (broken into lumps) to every pint of juice. Stir, and when settled put the jar into a pan of water. Let it simmer and skim it. Let it cool, then bottle it. When cold it will be fine and thick like strained honey newly prepared.

Red Currant Jelly

Put all the stems off the currants and stew them gently so as to draw out all the juice. Strain it, and to each pint of juice allow one pound of sugar. Then boil from three-quarters of an hour to an hour until it jellies.

Georgiana, Countess of Dudley, *The Dudley Book of Cookery & Household Recipes*, 1910

Superlative Red Currant Jelly

Strip carefully from the stems some quite ripe currants of the finest quality, and mix with them an equal weight of good sugar reduced to powder; boil these together quickly for exactly eight minutes, keep them stirred all the time, and clear off the scum—which will be very abundant—as it rises; then turn the preserve into a very clean sieve, and put into small jars the jelly which runs through it, and which will be delicious in flavour, and of the brightest colour. It should be carried immediately . . . to an extremely cool but not a damp place, and left there until perfectly cold. The currants which remain in the sieve make an excellent jam, particularly if only part of the jelly be taken from them.

Currants, 3 lbs; sugar, 3 lbs; 8 minutes.

Jelly of Ripe Gooseberries
(*Excellent*)

Take the tops and stalks from a gallon or more of well-flavoured ripe red gooseberries, and keep them stirred gently over a clear fire until they have yielded all their juice, which should then be poured off without pressing the fruit, and passed first through a fine sieve, and afterwards through a double muslin-strainer or a jelly-bag. Next weigh it, and to every three pounds add one of white currant juice, which has previously been prepared in the same way; boil these quickly for a quarter of an hour, then draw them from the fire and stir to them half their weight of good sugar; when this is dissolved, boil the jelly for six minutes longer, skim it thoroughly, and pour it into jars or moulds. If a very large quantity be made, a few minutes of additional boiling must be given to it *before* the sugar is added.

Juice of red gooseberries, 3 lbs; juice of white currants, 1 lb: 15 minutes. Sugar, 2 lbs: 6 minutes.

Obs. The same proportion of red currant juice, mixed with that of the gooseberries, makes an exceedingly nice jelly.

Eliza Acton, *Modern Cookery for Private Families*, 1845

ELDERBERRY KETCHUP OR PONTACK SAUCE

Pick a quart of ripe elderberries, place in a stone jar and cover with vinegar, cook in a slow oven for three hours, then strain, and to the liquor add some shallots, a blade of mace, a few cloves, half lb sugar and a few peppers. Simmer gently for an hour then strain and bottle well.

Lucy H. Yates, *The Country Housewife's Book*, 1934

APPLE JELLY

Half a bushel (i.e. the quantity of fruit that would fill a four-gallon container or two usual-sized buckets) of good-looking apples, pare and core. Cover them with cold water and put on to simmer till cooked. Then press through a jelly bag, and to each pint of juice allow three-quarters of a pound of crushed white sugar. Boil up well from three-quarters of an hour to an hour until it jellies.

CRAB APPLE JELLY

Wash the crab apples and drain them (you need not peel or core). Cover with cold water, and let them gently boil until they break, but do not allow them to become "pulpy", then pass the juice through a jelly bag. To each pint of juice allow one pound of sugar. Boil quickly until it jellies. It should be clear and red in colour. This is good for sore throats.

Georgiana, Countess of Dudley, *The Dudley Book of Cookery & Household Recipes*, 1910

QUINCE JELLY

Select very ripe fruit; cut it into slices; peel and pip these, and throw them into a basin of fresh water.

Then put them into a preserving-pan with three and a half pints of water per lb of quinces, and cook them without touching them. This done, transfer them to a sieve, and let them drain. Return the juice to the pan, together with twelve oz of loaf-sugar per lb; dissolve the sugar; and set the whole to cook on a fierce fire, meanwhile skimming with care, until the "nappe" stage is almost reached.

As soon as the jelly is cooked, strain in through a piece of muslin stretched over a basin; and by this means a perfectly clear jelly will be obtained.

A. Escoffier, *A Guide to Modern Cookery*, 1926

ROWAN JELLY

(*Old Family Recipe*)

Rowan berries, apples, water, sugar.

Gather your rowan berries when almost ripe. Remove the stalks and wash and drain the berries. Put them in a preserving-pan with enough cold water to float them well. Let them simmer for about forty minutes or until the water is red and the berries are quite soft. Strain off the juice, being careful not to press the fruit in the least. Measure the juice and return it to the pan. Add sugar in the proportion of a pound to each pint of juice. Boil rapidly for half an hour or until some of it sets quickly on a plate when cold. Skim it well, pour it into small pots, and tie down quickly.

If you allow pound for pound of apple juice to rowan juice you will get a delightful jelly. Allow a pound of sugar to each pint of apple juice.

Rowan jelly is an excellent accompaniment to grouse, venison and saddle of mutton.

F. Marian McNeill, *The Scots Kitchen*, 1989 edition

Dressings in Northern Italy

There is great virtue in the herbs of the field, both as edibles and as fuel. Roast your quail over dried vine-branches, and acknowledge that there is wisdom in the latter part of the statement. For your stew of rabbit or boar, wild thyme is desirable both inside and outside the pot, or under the grill. I have found a few pungent juniper-berries an excellent addition to a civet de sanglier. And these two, thyme and juniper, are the only things that make goat-flesh tolerable. Of other herbs, cherish the dandelion, king of salad meats; make use of wild sorrel to give a refreshing acidity to sauce or soup, and the olive, wherever procurable, green or brown and dripping with oil, to add a zest reminiscent of more epicurean feasts.

Guy Cadogan Rothery, *The Badminton Magazine*, 1897

——— Fried Breadcrumbs an Accompaniment to ——— Roast Pheasants, Partridges, and Grouse

Grate some stale bread, and if not very fine shake the crumbs through a colander so as to lie lightly in the dish. Melt a slice of butter in a frying pan, and fry the crumbs till all are well and equally coloured, stirring them to prevent burning, then well drain and dry them on paper, or a cloth spread upon a sieve. If preferred, the crumbs may be browned very gently in a cool or a Dutch oven, without butter. They are easily removed with a slice.

J. H. Walsh, F.R.C.S., *The British Cookery Book*, 1864

——————— Recipe for Salad Dressing ———————

Take the yolks of two fresh eggs entirely free from the whites with a dessertspoonful of French mustard, and stir until amalgamated. Gradually to this add drop by drop Lucca salad oil, about a fourth of a wine bottle; to this add a few drops of Worcester sauce, tarragon and vinegar, castor sugar and salts. Finally add half a pint of cream. Placed in a stoppered bottle, this will keep for a month or longer.

Georgiana, Countess of Dudley, *The Dudley Book of Cookery & Household Recipes*, 1910

The Poet's Receipt For Salad

Two large potatoes, passed through kitchen sieve
Unwonted softness to the salad give;
Of mordent mustard, add a single spoon,
Distrust the condiment which bites so soon;
But deem it not, thou man of herbs, a fault,
To add a double quantity of salt;
Three times the spoon with oil of Lucca crown,
And once with vinegar, procured from town;
True flavour needs it, and your poet begs
The pounded yellow of two well-boiled eggs;
Let onion atoms lurk within the bowl
And, scarce suspected, animate the whole;
And lastly, in the flavoured compound toss
A magic teaspoon of anchovy sauce:
Then, though green turtle fail, though venison's tough,
And ham and turkey are not boiled enough,
Serenely full, the epicure may say—
Fate cannot harm me,—I have dined today.

Rev. Sydney Smith, 1771–1845

(Quoted by Eliza Acton in *Modern Cookery for Private Families*. Mrs Acton comments, "We would not venture to deviate by a word from the original, but we would suggest that the mixture forms almost a substitute for salad, instead of a mere dressing. It is, however, an admirable compound for those to whom the slight flavouring of onion is not an objection.")

Sauces

SAUCES are legion, as are books about them, be they monographs on the subject or cookery classics such as Escoffier's *Guide to Modern Cookery*, which gives instructions for more than a hundred sauces. For this reason I have not included the many sauces which are well defined elsewhere.

Sauces which seem to me appropriate for particular dishes are listed along with their subject, but there are a few which should be mentioned separately because they are not well known and have special merit for game in general.

HOT MEAT SAUCES

There is only one sauce which may be called the best for everybody, at all times and upon all occasions: it is a healthy appetite. The next best sauce is wine, but only in the case of food which is perfect of its kind, neither tasteless nor too tasty, neither too dry nor too watery. A grilled sole, for instance, with just a pat of fresh butter, does not require any other sauce than a bottle of Bockstein, Scharzberg or Eitelsbacher. A young partridge, roasted and served with just the fat and blood that oozed out of its plump body, needs no better sauce than a bottle of Chateau Ausone or of Musigny. But such cases are exceptions. As a rule meat and poultry, and more particularly fish and vegetables, require a little help, and the best assistance they can get is that which a well-chosen sauce will render.

André L. Simon, *The Art of Good Living*, 1930

— Christopher North's Own Sauce for Many Meats —

Throw into a small basin a heaped saltspoonful of good cayenne pepper, in very fine powder, and half the quantity of salt; add a small dessertspoonful of well-refined, pounded, and sifted sugar; mix these thoroughly; then pour in a tablespoonful of the strained juice of a fresh lemon, two of Harvey's Sauce, a teaspoonful of the very best mushroom catsup (or of cavice), and three tablespoonsful, or a small wineglassful, of port wine. Heat the sauce by placing the basin in a saucepan of boiling water, or turn it into a jar, and place this in the water. Serve it directly it is ready with geese or ducks, tame or wild; roast pork, venison, fawn, a grilled blade-bone, or any other broil. A slight flavour of garlic or escalot vinegar may be given to it at pleasure. Some persons use it with fish. It is good cold; and, if bottled directly it is made, may be stored for several days. It is the better for being mixed some hours before it is served. The proportion of cayenne may be doubled when a very pungent sauce is desired.

Good cayenne pepper in fine powder, 1 heaped saltspoonful; salt, half as much; pounded sugar, 1 small dessertspoonful; strained lemon juice, 1 tablespoonful; Harvey's Sauce, 2 tablespoonsful; best mushroom catsup (or cavice), 1 teaspoonful; port wine, 3 tablespoonsful, or small wineglassful. (Little escalot, or garlic-vinegar at pleasure.)

Obs. This sauce is exceedingly good when mixed with the brown gravy of a hash or stew, or with that which is served with game or other dishes.

Eliza Acton, *Modern Cookery for Private Families*, 1845

— Our Own Sauce for Game (or Orange Gravy) —

A half pint of claret, and the same quantity of good brown-gravy. Make the gravy boil, and put the wine to it, with pepper, salt, cayenne, and the strained juice of two seville oranges, or one orange and a lemon. Let them simmer for a few minutes, and, pouring some over the game, serve the rest very hot in a tureen.

Margaret Dods, *The Cook & Housewife's Manual*, 1870 edition

Excellent Sauce for Game or Meat

Mix thoroughly together two tablespoonfuls of Harvey Sauce, one glass of port wine, one dessertspoonful of white sugar, one dessertspoonful of mushroom ketchup, one tablespoonful of lemon juice, half a teaspoonful of salt, half a teaspoonful of cayenne pepper. Place the vessel in which it is made into a saucepan of boiling water, and heat the sauce gradually. Do not let it boil.

Sauce for Grilled Game

One tablespoonful of mustard, one tablespoonful of salad oil, a little Harvey Sauce, cayenne pepper and salt to taste. Mix all together and baste the game, and grill it again, then add the remains of the sauce with a little glaze.

Susan, Duchess of Somerset, *The Duchess Cookery Book*, 1934

Madeira Sauce
for Entrées of Meat, Poultry and Game

Ingredients. Half a pint of Espagnole sauce, quarter of a pint of good gravy, 1 oz of meat glaze, 1 glass of Madeira or sherry, salt and pepper.

Method. Simmer the sauce, gravy and wine until well reduced. Season to taste, put in the meat glaze, stir until it is dissolved, then strain the sauce, and use as required.

Time. About half an hour.

Red Currant Sauce
For Puddings, Venison, Hare, etc.

Ingredients. A small jar of red currant jelly, 1 small glass of port.

Method. Put the wine and jelly into a small saucepan, let them slowly come to the boil, and serve when the jelly is dissolved.

Time. About 5 minutes.

Mrs Beeton's *All-About Cookery*, c. 1930

Good Bread Sauce for Game

Put one pint of new milk to boil with one onion and a few white peppercorns. Let it simmer for a while; steam it, and return it to the fire. Add two handfuls of breadcrumbs, one gill of cream, pepper and salt and serve hot.

A Good Chasseur Sauce for Game

Peel and mince six medium-sized mushrooms; heat half an ounce of butter and as much olive oil in a vegetable pan. Put in the mushrooms and fry them quickly until they are slightly browned; then add a teaspoonful of minced shallots and immediately remove half the butter. Pour half a pint of white wine and one glass of liqueur brandy into the stewpan; reduce this liquid to one-half and finish the sauce with half a pint of half glaze, a quarter of a pint of tomato sauce and one tablespoonful of meat glaze. Set to boil for five minutes more and finish with a teaspoonful of chopped parsley.

Georgiana, Countess of Dudley, *A Second Dudley Book of Cookery*, 1914

Grill Sauce

Half a teaspoonful of mustard, one tablespoonful Harvey Sauce, one ounce of glaze, a few drops of salad oil, a small piece of butter about the size of a walnut, a pinch of black pepper, of cayenne, and of salt. Mix all up on a plate, put the meat to be grilled in this mixture and broil before a clear fire for a few seconds. Place the remainder of the sauce into a small stewpan to heat but not boil; dish the grill, pour the sauce over and serve.

Red Wine Sauce

Half a pint of red wine. Let it boil with a small pinch of pepper and a very small quantity of shallot until there is only about half a cupful left in the saucepan. Then add three tablespoonfuls of very rich brown stock. Let it simmer slowly. Add butter and a pinch of salt to taste, stirring it with a spoon. The sauce must then be passed through a cloth.

Georgiana, Countess of Dudley, *The Dudley Book of Cookery & Household Recipes*, 1910

PIQUANTE SAUCE

Chop up a small onion finely, and put it into a saucepan with two tablespoonfuls of wine vinegar. Let the vinegar boil until it has nearly disappeared, then add half a pint of ordinary brown sauce and a tablespoonful each of coarsely chopped gherkins and capers cut in half. Simmer together for five minutes or so, and it is ready.

Ambrose Heath, *From Creel to Kitchen*, 1939

WHITE MUSHROOM SAUCE

Cut off the stems closely from half a pint of small button mushrooms; clean them with a little salt and a bit of flannel, and throw them into cold water, slightly salted, as they are done; drain them well, or dry them in a soft cloth and throw them into half a pint of boiling béchamel, or of white sauce made with very fresh milk, or thin cream, thickened with a tablespoonful of flour and two ounces of butter. Simmer the mushrooms from ten to twenty minutes, or until they are quite tender, and dish the sauce, which should be properly seasoned with salt, mace, and cayenne.

Eliza Acton, *Modern Cookery for Private Families*, 1845

MUSHROOM SAUCE

Skin and slice 2 or 3 large mushrooms and place in a quarter pint milk. Cook. Add 1 oz margarine, half oz flour rolled together. Re-boil, add pinch salt and serve.

Nell Heaton & André Simon, *A Calendar of Food & Wine*, 1949

HOT FISH SAUCES

ANCHOVY SAUCE

This is a white (melted butter) sauce, to which anchovy essence has been added in the proportion you like.

A richer sauce is made as follows: Melt two ounces of butter, add an ounce of flour, moisten with three-quarters of a pint of fresh cream, season with salt and pepper, and bring to the boil. Finish at the last moment with a dessertspoonful of anchovy essence, or, better, with two ounces of anchovy butter.

CAPER SAUCE

This is a white (melted butter) sauce to which capers are added in the proportion of a good tablespoonful of capers to half a pint of the sauce.

Ambrose Heath, *From Creel to Kitchen*, 1939

PARSLEY SAUCE

Take a handful of parsley, wash well, chop finely. Place in a saucepan and cover with boiling water. Boil for 5 minutes. Add half oz butter and a dessertspoonful vinegar, and serve very hot.

LOBSTER SAUCE

Make a white sauce and add pieces of diced lobster.

White Sauce. Make a white sauce by blending together in a small saucepan over a gentle heat, without discolouring, 1 oz margarine and 1 oz flour. Add half pint milk, stir till boiling. Boil for 2 minutes if for coating. Add either sugar or pepper and salt.

Nell Heaton & André Simon, A *Calendar of Food & Wine*, 1949

SHRIMP SAUCE

Ingredients. Half a pint of white sauce, quarter of a pint of picked shrimps, 1 teaspoonful of anchovy-essence, a few drops of lemon-juice, cayenne.

Method. The fish stock required for the white sauce may be obtained by simmering the shrimp shells in milk and water. Add the shrimps, anchovy-essence, lemon-juice and cayenne to the hot sauce. Cover the saucepan, and let it stand for a few minutes where the contents cannot boil, then serve.

Time. About 40 minutes.

Quantity. About half pint.

Horseradish Sauce or Cream (Hot) for Boiled Fish or Roast Meat

Ingredients. Three-quarters oz of flour, 1 oz of butter, three-quarters pint of milk or cream, 2 tablespoonfuls of finely-grated horseradish, 1 teaspoonful of vinegar, a pinch of salt, half a teaspoonful of sugar.

Method. Blend the flour with the butter, boil the milk or cream, and add it to the butter and flour; stir over the fire and boil for about 5 minutes, taking great care not to let it curdle. Pass through a tammy-cloth or very fine strainer. Add the horeseradish, salt and vinegar, and mix well. Serve as hot as possible.

Time. From 20 to 30 minutes.

Quantity. About three-quarters pint.

Mrs Beeton, *All-About Cookery*, c. 1930

Dr Kitchiner's Fish Sauce Superlative, a Store-Sauce

A pint of claret, a pint of mushroom-catsup, and half a pint of walnut pickle; four ounces of pounded anchovy, an ounce of fresh lemon-peel pared thin, and the same quantity of eschalot and scraped horseradish: an ounce of black pepper and allspice, and a drachm [⅛ oz] of cayenne, or three of curry-powder, with a drachm of celery-seed. Infuse these, in a wide-mouthed bottle closely stopped, for a fortnight, and shake the mixture every day; then strain and bottle it for use. A large spoonful of this stirred into a quarter-pint of thickened melted butter "makes", says the Doctor, "an admirable extemporaneous sauce".

──────────── THE OLD ADMIRAL'S SAUCE ────────────

Chop an anchovy, a dozen capers, and four eschalots or rocamboles [Spanish garlic]; simmer these in melted butter till the anchovy dissolves and season with pepper and salt; and when ready, add the juice of a lemon and grated nutmeg.

Margaret Dods, *The Cook & Housewife's Manual*, 1870 edition

──────────── SORREL SAUCE ────────────

Throw a bunch of young sorrel leaves into boiling, slightly salted water, and boil fast until tender. Fast boiling conserves the vitamins better than slow boiling. Drain the sorrel, chop the leaves finely or rub them through a sieve. Work plenty of butter or cream into the purée, thicken with brown roux and season with salt, pepper and a little sugar if liked. Add fish stock as required, boil for four or five minutes, stirring well, and the sauce is ready.

──────────── GOOSEBERRY SAUCE ────────────

Cook one pound of green gooseberries and some finely minced chives over a slow heat with two tablespoonfuls of water. When the juice begins to flow increase the heat. Cook until soft. Add one teaspoonful of nutmeg, pepper, salt, a teaspoonful of sugar to take off the sharpness, and beat in by degrees three tablespoonfuls of butter. Finish with a little lemon juice.

Margaret Dods, *The Cook & Housewife's Manual*, 1870 edition

COLD SAUCES FOR MEAT AND FISH

Harveys

Two Harveys had a separate wish
To shine in separate stations;
The one invented sauce for fish,
The other, meditations.

While thus each one his talents tried
For living and for dying,
This relishes a sole when fried
That saves a soul from frying.

Fores's *Sporting Notes and Sketches*, 1898

ENGLISH SAUCE FOR SALAD, COLD MEAT, OR COLD FISH

The first essential for a smooth, well-made English salad dressing is to have the yolks of the eggs used for it sufficiently hard to be reduced easily to a perfect paste. They should be boiled at least fifteen minutes, and should have become *quite* cold before they are taken from the shells; they should also be well covered with water when they are cooked, or some parts of them will be tough, and will spoil the appearance of the sauce by rendering it lumpy, unless they be worked through a sieve, a process which is always better avoided if possible. To a couple of yolks broken up and mashed to a paste with the back of a wooden spoon, add a small saltspoonful of salt, a large one of pounded sugar, a few grains of fine cayenne, and a teaspoonful of cold water; mix these well, and stir to them by degrees a quarter of a pint of sweet cream; throw in next, stirring the sauce briskly, a tablespoonful of strong chilli vinegar, and add as much common or French vinegar as will acidulate the mixture agreeably. A tablespoonful of either will be sufficient for many tastes, but it is easy to increase the proportion when more is liked. Six tablespoonsful of olive oil, of the purest quality, may be substituted for the cream: it should be added in very small portions to the other ingredients, and stirred briskly until the sauce resembles custard. When this is used, the water should be omitted. The piquancy of this preparation—which is very delicate, made by the directions just given—may be heightened by the addition of a little eschalot vinegar, Harvey's sauce, essence of anchovies, French mustard or tarragon vinegar; or by bruising with the eggs a morsel of garlic, half the size of a hazel-nut: it should always, however, be rendered as appropriate as may be to the dish with which it is to be served.

Obs. As we have before had occasion to remark, garlic, when very sparingly and judiciously used, imparts a remarkable fine savour to a sauce or gravy, and neither a strong nor a coarse one, as it does when used in larger quantities. The veriest morsel . . . is sufficient to give this agreeable piquancy, but unless the proportion be extremely small, the effect will be quite different.

Eliza Acton, Modern Cookery for Private Families, 1845

CHRISTOPHER NORTH'S FISH SAUCE

Shepherd. I never look at the sea without lamenting the backward state of its agriculture. Were every eatable land animal extinc', the human race could dine and soup out o' the ocean till a' eternity.

Tickler. No fish-sauce equal to the following: Ketchup-mustard—cayenne pepper—butter amalgamated on your plate proprio manu, each man according to his own proportions. Yetholm Ketchup made by the gipsies. Mushrooms for ever—damn walnuts.

Christopher North, Noctes Ambrosianae, 1888

HORSERADISH SAUCE (COLD)
FOR HOT OR COLD ROAST MEAT

Ingredients. About I oz of finely grated horseradish, 1 gill of thick cream or unsweetened condensed milk, 1 to 2 tablespoonfuls of white wine vinegar, 1 teaspoonful of castor sugar, a little powdered mustard, pepper and salt.

Method. Put the horseradish in a basin, add the sugar, mustard, salt and pepper; moisten with vinegar, stir in the cream or condensed milk gradually. Serve cold.

Time. From 10 to 15 minutes.

Quantity. About one-third pint.

Mrs Beeton, All-About Cookery, c. 1930

GREEN SAUCE

Blanch in boiling salted water for ten minutes, watercress leaves, young spinach leaves, chervil, tarragon, parsley and chives, about two or three ounces in all. Drain these herbs, plunge them in cold water, and squeeze them in a cloth so as to extract as much moisture as possible from them. Now pound them in a mortar, pass them through a very fine sieve or tammy-cloth, and add this purée to three-quarters of a pint of mayonnaise.

Ambrose Heath, *Madame Prunier's Fish Cookery Book*, 1938

——— How to Make a Good Mayonnaise Sauce ———

Take the yolks of three fresh eggs free from the whites. Put in a basin, with a pinch of pepper, salt and mustard. With a wooden spoon work this gently; then add, drop by drop, a pint or more of the very best olive oil (virgin oil from Negre Grasse is by far the best); stir this well, then add, drop by drop, a very small quantity of tarragon vinegar. The sauce should be smooth and very thick.

Georgiana, Countess of Dudley, *The Dudley Book of Cookery & Household Recipes*, 1910

——— Cold Mayonnaise Sauce à la Farquhar ———

Take the yolks of three fresh eggs, free from the whites. Put them in a basin with a pinch of pepper, salt and mustard. Work this gently with a wooden spoon; then add drop by drop a pint or more of the very best olive oil. Stir this well; then add drop by drop a very small quantity of tarragon vinegar. The sauce should be smooth and very thick. Take two or more tablespoonfuls of the above, according to the quantity of sauce required, and add to it about half a gill or more of whipped cream. Mix lightly and add to it four or more small onions, cut into halves. Allow them to remain in the sauce for about an hour to flavour it; then remove the onions. Mix the sauce again very lightly, and sprinkle with a pinch of very finely chopped parsley and chervil.

This sauce is excellent served with grilled or spatchcock chicken or game, or mutton cutlets breadcrumbed and served on a grid.

Georgiana, Countess of Dudley, *A Second Dudley Book of Cookery*, 1914

——— Cumberland Sauce ———

Three oranges, one lemon, one tablespoonful of Worcester Sauce, one tablespoonful of Harvey Sauce, two tablespoonsful of red currant jelly, a little Bengal Club chutnee, and a wineglassful of claret or port wine. Put the wine and jelly into a small stewpan to boil for five minutes, then add the chutnee and sauces. Squeeze in the juice of the three oranges and the lemon, then strain and serve cold, adding the rind of two oranges finely cut à la julienne, taking care to cut away the white inside part of the peel.

Sauce Bignon
for Cold Fish, Salad, or White Meat

Chop up very fine two teaspoonfuls of chervil, the same of tarragon leaves, if possible, if not half a teaspoonful of vinegar and two teaspoons of chives. Mix with these two tablespoons of the best oil and half a spoon of malt vinegar.

Georgiana, Countess of Dudley, *The Dudley Book of Cookery & Household Recipes*, 1910

A La Carte

Dinner at New College

Aug. 17, 1763. Dined in Hall at the High Table upon a neck of Venison and a Breast made into Pasty, a Ham and Fowls and two Pies. It is a Venison Feast which we have once a year about this time . . . 2 Bucks one year, and 1 Buck another year is always sent from Whaddon Chase and divided between the Wardens, the Senior Fellows, and us.

Dinner with the Bishop of Norwich

Sep. 4, 1783. There were 20 of us at the Table and a very elegant Dinner the Bishop gave us. We had 2 Courses of 20 Dishes each Course, and a Dessert after of 20 dishes. Madeira, red and white Wines. The first Course amongst many other things were 2 Dishes of prodigious fine stewed Carp and Tench, and a fine Haunch of Venison. Amongst the second Course a fine Turkey Poult, Partridges, Pidgeons and Sweatmeats. Dessert—amongst other things, Mulberries, Melon, Currants, Peaches, Nectarines and Grapes.

The King's Head, Norwich

Dec. 19, 1785. Supper being just going in for the Family I joined them, and there met with the best Supper I ever met with at an Inn. Hashed fowl, veal collopes, a fine Woodcock, a Couple of

Whistling Plovers, a real Teal of the small kind and hot Apple Pye.

Rev. James Woodforde, *Diary of a Country Parson*

Note on Parson Woodforde. The diaries of The Reverend James Woodforde (1740–1803), which cover the years 1758–1802, were unknown until discovered early in the present century. When they were published, he was quickly recognised as one of the great diarists. A country parson, first in Somerset and then in Norfolk, he recorded the annals of country people, rich and poor, in vivid detail. That detail extended to the inclusion, almost invariably in each entry, of what he had eaten that day.

An Old Flame Comes to Luncheon

Decorate the table with Rosemary and Love-lies-bleeding.

Menu

Sole in Aspic
Partridge (shot through the head)
Grape Sauce (rather sour)
Passion Fruit Frappé
Coffee
Cigarettes

Rose Henniker Heaton, *The Perfect Hostess*, 1931

Provisions for Coaches

During cold weather the interior of the coach should be well filled with earthenware vessels containing such provender as hot-pot, hare soup, mullagatawny, lobster à l'Americaine, curried rabbit . . . with the material for heating these. Such cold viands as game pie, pressed beef, boar's head, foie gras (truffled), plain truffles (to be steamed and served with buttered toast), anchovies, etc.

Edward Spencer, *Cakes & Ale*, 1897

Sportsmen's Inns

I have also a dour reminiscence of a long and lonely evening passed at Bettyhill Hotel, at the mouth of the Naver. No one else was staying there, and not a newspaper in the place; a hunt for books revealed three: their titles were "Early Graves", "Elijah and Ahab", and "A Candle Lighted by the Lord" . . . I likewise remember that on arriving at the Thurso Hotel an inquiry as to lunch elicited from a black satin-clad manageress with very shiny black ringlets and a big bunch of scarlet geraniums in front of her dress, and who "creaked" with every breath, "Lunch, sir? Yes, sir! In the course of a few minutes I will serve you with a nice little cold collation in the Salle à Manger; pray leave it to me, sir." This high-sounding description of a cold shoulder of tough mutton little better than an already picked bone and some soapy cheese has always made me laugh whenever recalled to mind.

Augustus Grimble, *More Leaves from My Game Book*, 1917

Precautions at Inns

If the beer is sour, and he does not choose to be troubled with carrying bottles of other beverage, he is provided with a little carbonate of soda, which will correct the acid; a little nutmeg or powdered ginger, to take off the unpleasant taste; and, with a spoonful of brown sugar and a toast, he will make tolerably palatable that which, before, was scarcely good enough to quench the thirst.

Lt-Col. P. Hawker, *Instructions to Young Sportsmen*, 1814

Dinner with Mr Stanley Sterling

Mr Facey Romford—lured, perhaps, by the fame of Mr Stanley Sterling's nutty sherry, ruby port, and comfortable *menage* generally—has come over to Rosemount to be handy for the meet on the morrow . . . Mr Stanley Sterling did not attempt side-dishes, but let his cook concentrate her talents upon a few general favourites. Hence the ox-tail soup was always beautifully clear and hot, the crimped-cod and oyster sauce excellent, while the boiled fowls and ruddy ham ran a close race with the four-year-old leg of roast mutton, leaving the relish they give for the "sweet or dry" to support their claims for preference. Beer and mealy potatoes accompanied the solids and macaroni and mince-pies followed in due course. A bottle of Beaujolais circulated with the cheese. They had then all dined to their hearts content.

As Romford chucked his napkin in a sort of happy-go-lucky way over his left shoulder, he thought how much better it was than any of the grand spreads he had seen. Grace being said, the plate-warmer was then taken from the fire, the horseshoe-table sub-stituted, and each man prepared to make himself comfortable according to his own peculiar fashion.

R. S. Surtees, *Mr Facey Romford's Hounds*, 1865

Christmas at New College

Dec. 25, 1773. We had for dinner, two fine Codds boiled with fryed Souls round them and oyster sauce, a fine sirloin of Beef roasted, some peas soup and an orange Pudding for the first course, for the second, we had a lease of Wild Ducks rosted, a fore Quarter of Lamb and Sallad and mince pies.

Rev. James Woodforde, *Diary of a Country Parson*, 1758–1802

Colonel Thornton's Christmas Dinner, 1821

On Christmas Day, 1821, the newspapers announced Thornton's death. He wrote to a friend contradicting the report.

My honest Brother Sportsman

This is Christmas-day, dedicated by me, from my youth, to gaiety and reasonable hospitality . . .

In health, no man can be more hearty . . . stomach invincible,—always an appetite. Eat three times a day. Tea, muffins, and grated hung beef at nine;—at two, roasted game or cockscombs, and about a pint of the finest white Burgundy. Dinner at five, and then a bottle of wine, about three or four glasses of spirits and water rather weak—then to bed . . .

P.S. Dec. 26. I find by the papers that I died after a short illness, much lamented, and at Paris. However that may be, I gave a dinner yesterday to a dozen sportsmen: we had roast beef, plum pudding, Yorkshire goose-pie, and sat up singing till two this morning. At twelve we had two broiled fowls, gizzards, etc., and finished a bottle of old rum in punch.

Pierce Egan, Sporting Anecdotes, 1820

A Poor Day

April 5, 1793. Called this morning at Mr Carys, and found the old Gentleman almost at his last gasp. Totally senseless with rattlings in his Throat. Dinner today boiled beef and Rabbit rosted. Poor old Mr Carys died this Afternoon.

Rev. James Woodforde, Diary of a Country Parson, 1758–1802

Causes and Consequences of Indigestion

Generally, depend on it, missing means indigestion. Your friend prepares you for the day's work with a dinner of Chablis, oysters, turbot and oyster sauce (caper sauce if he is a man of taste), patties, croquets, cutlets à la this, that, and the other. Next comes the joint and turkey, game, rich gravy, toast, fried crumbs and sauces, creams, jellies, whips, trifles, and syllabubs, rich puddings, iced puddings, and what not to be succeeded by Stilton cheese and the pie of Strasburg; then dried cherries, tough figs, grapes ad lib., a sponge cake, crystallised fruit, Spanish plums and roasted chestnuts, to say nothing of the hock, champagne (dry), sherry, claret, and that little glass of liqueur, which is supposed to be plenary absolution to the drinker for all his weakness and profane trifling with his liver and digestion.

Who wonders that next morning . . . I shoot too quickly with my first barrel, that my aim is oblique, and that Helvellyn, the solicitor . . . spreads damaging reports of my qualifications as a shot and whispers to his engrossing clerk, who carries his cartridges in the professional blue bag behind his master, "that Hidstone is no great shakes, he'll take his affidavit".

. . . I will give my readers a carte of a dinner, and some of the results, to exemplify what a liberal host will do to entertain his guests, and how they performed next day.

I went to look over the kennels of a country magistrate some time last year, and to share in two days shooting . . . The first day I had nothing to complain of, as my repast was simple, and I hope the second was moderate; but here's the carte, which I preserve as a curiosity, and some day I will have it framed:

Soups.	Turtle, Jardinière, clear soup, sherry and Sauterne.
Fish.	Turbot, lobster sauce. Wines, Château Yquem, Hochheiner, sherry.
Removes.	Haunch of venison, braised turkey, truffled, boned and stuffed with tongue. Wines, St Julien, La Rose.
Entrées.	Vol-au-Vent with oysters, partridges à la Périgord, sweetbreads à la Monarque, cutlets à la Jardinière. Champagne, Cliquot & Moët, sparkling hock. Punch à la Romain.
Second Course.	Roast pheasants, Woodcocks. Wines, Burgundy, Chambertin, Clos Vougeot.
Removes.	Paté de foie gras, iced pudding.
Entremets.	Chantilly cake, Charlotte Russe, Pineapple jelly, meringue à la Parisienne.
Dessert.	Grapes, pineapples, apples (Golden Pippin), petites pommes d'Assis, pears, oranges, four crystallised fruits, two cakes, cream ice (au café), water ice (lemon).
Wines.	Sherry; Lafitte, '58; Margaux, '58; Latour, '58; Port, '20.

I partook of a selection of these viands, and that but sparingly. Next day, however, I wasn't up to the mark. Here is my score:

Pheasants, 001000011001011110111
Woodcocks, 01
Hares, 01100010001100101110
Rabbits, none.

"Idstone", *The "Idstone" Papers*, 1872

Soups

SOUP can be the preface to a meal, a substantial part of it, or the meal itself. A consommé stimulates the appetite for what is to come while, by contrast, the Poacher's Soup of Meg Merrilies will go far to satisfy the hungriest.

Margaret Dods called soup the safest foundation to the principal repast of the day, whether it were a Cottage or a Cabinet dinner. The French, she said, took the lead of all European people in soups and broths and the Scots ranked second. That, she said, was probably due to the long and close alliance with France, a nation which was always most profoundly skilled in the mysteries of the soup pot.

There is no doubt the Scots still excel at soup-making, and the wide choice of game in the country makes for infinite variety. If you are suspicious of the quality of food on a menu, be it in hostelry or hospital, at least in Scotland choose the soup, for you are unlikely to be disappointed.

GAME CONSOMMÉ

The necks, breasts, and shoulders of venison and of hare, old wild rabbits, old pheasants, and old partridges may be used in the production of game consommés. An ordinary consommé may likewise be made, in which half the beef can be replaced by veal, and to which may be added, while clarifying, a succulent game essence. This last method is even preferable when dealing with feathered game, but in either case it is essential that the meat used should be half-roasted beforehand, in order to strengthen the fumet.

The formula that I give below must therefore only be looked upon as a model, necessarily alterable according to the resources at one's disposal, the circumstances, and the end in view.

Quantities for making Four Quarts of Plain Game Consommé

3 lb of neck, shoulder or breast of venison

1½ lb of hare trimmings

1 old pheasant or 2 partridges

4 oz of sliced carrots, browned in butter

½ lb of mushrooms, likewise browned in butter

1 medium-sized leek and 2 sticks of celery

1 bunch of herbs with extra thyme and bay leaves

1 onion, oven-browned, with 2 cloves stuck into it

Liquor. 5½ quarts of water.

Seasoning. 1 oz of salt and a few peppercorns, these to be added ten minutes previous to straining the consommé.

Time allowed for cooking. Three hours.

Mode of Procedure. Proceed in exactly the same way as for ordinary consommés, taking care only to half-roast the meat . . . before putting it in the stewpan.

A. Escoffier, *A Guide to Modern Cookery*, 1926

Venison Consommé

Take six or seven pounds of the knuckle-end of a haunch of venison, three pounds of knuckle of veal and one soup fowl. Place the meat in a stockpot. Cover it with cold water. Let this come to the boil. Skim off the sediment which rises, then add two leeks, two carrots, two onions, a bunch of parsley and a little salt. Let boil gently for six or seven hours, strain and, when cold, remove all fat and place again on fire in a large pan. When lukewarm, add four pounds of the gravy part of a haunch, which has been passed through a mincing machine or mixed with one quart of water. Add to this, one carrot, two leeks, a little parsley and celery cut into small pieces. Place on fire and allow it to boil, stirring all the time. When it boils, draw to side of stove and allow it to simmer gently. Roast the fowl and place it in the pot. Let all cook for five or six hours, then strain through a soup-cloth which has been wrung through hot water to remove all taint of soap. Take care that the consommé is clear and bright.

Some very small quenelles of venison should be served in the consommé.

Georgiana, Countess of Dudley, *A Second Dudley Book of Cookery*, 1914

GAME SOUP

This soup can be made with the remains of cold game. Boil the remains, removing the skin, for about three-quarters of an hour with a few carrots and onions, some sticks of celery and a bouquet of parsley, thyme and bayleaf. Then pass it through a fine sieve, and pound up the pieces of flesh in a mortar and pass them through a sieve too. Mix them with just a little very finely grated stale white breadcrumbs and mix them carefully with the soup. Bind with some cream at the last minute, and serve with fried croutons.

GROUSE SOUP

A sportsman's recipe. Three-parts roast an old grouse, cut off the breast fillets, take the rest of the meat from the bones and pound it in a mortar. Add this pounded meat to a pint and a half of stock rather strongly flavoured with celery, and meanwhile fry two ounces of fine oatmeal in the same amount of butter till it is a rich brown. Moisten this with stock till it is creamy, and then add it to the main stock. Simmer this for an hour and a half, strain it, season it, heat it again well through, and serve it with quenelles made with the pounded and sieved breast fillets.

CREOLE RABBIT SOUP

Cut two young rabbits into small pieces, and put them in a stewpan with two quarts of cold water. Chop up an onion and add it to the water, with a blade of mace and a bayleaf. Bring to the boil and simmer for two hours. Now add salt, pepper and cayenne pepper, and half a cupful of rice. Simmer for another hour, and when serving add a couple of tablespoonfuls of sherry.

Ambrose Heath, *Good Soups*, 1935

SUPERLATIVE GAME SOUP, OR VENISON SOUP

This soup is made of all sorts of black or red game, or of venison or wild rabbits. Skin the birds, carve and trim them neatly, and fry the pieces along with a few small slices of lean ham, sliced onions, carrots, and turnips, a little of each. Strain, and stew the meat gently for an hour in good fresh veal or beef stock-broth, with a head of celery cut in nice bits, a little minced parsley, and what seasonings you like. Very small steaks of venison may be fried, as the birds, and stewed in the broth; and if the stock is made of any venison trimmings, it will be an advantage both in flavour and strength. *Obs.* Jamaica pepper and cloves are suitable seasonings; celery, from its nutty flavour, is a proper vegetable for hare and game soups. Take out the ham before dishing.

POACHER'S SOUP
OR SOUP À LA MEG MERRILIES—SIMPLE AND ADMIRABLE

This savoury and highly-relishing Sylvan stew-soup may be made of any or every thing known by the name of game, if fresh. Take from two to four pounds of the trimmings or coarse parts of venison, shin of beef, or knuckles of lean scrag of good mutton—all fresh. If game is plentiful, use no meat. Break the bones, and boil this in five pints of water, with celery, a couple of carrots and turnips, four onions, a bunch of parsley, and a quarter-ounce of peppercorns, the larger portion Jamaican pepper. Strain this stock when it has simmered for three hours. Have ready cut-down a black-cock, or wood-cock, a pheasant, half a hare, or a rabbit, a brace of partridges or grouse, or one of each (whichever is obtained most easily—a mixture is best), and season the pieces with mixed spices. These may be floured and browned in the frying-pan; but as this is a process dictated by the eye as much as the palate, it is not necessary in making this soup. Put the cut game to the strained stock, with a dozen of small onions, a couple of heads of celery sliced, half a dozen peeled potatoes, or an ounce of rice-flour; and, when it boils, a very small white cabbage quartered; black pepper, allspice, and salt, to taste. Let the soup simmer till the game is tender, but not overdone; and lest it should, the vegetables may be boiled half an hour before the meat. *Obs.* This soup may be coloured and flavoured with red wine and two spoonfuls of mushroom catsup, and enriched with forecemeat balls; but we think it best plain. Foremeat balls are getting out of favour: they are considered indigestible, not without reason. Soup in which catsup is mixed should not be fully salted till the catsup is added, as it contains so much salt itself.

Margaret Dods, The Cook & Housewife's Manual, 1870 edition

Pheasant Soup

Half roast a brace of well-kept pheasants, and flour them rather thickly when they are first laid to the fire. As soon as they are nearly cold take all the flesh from the breasts, put it aside, and keep it covered from the air; carve down the remainder of the birds into joints, bruise the bodies thoroughly, and stew the whole gently from two to three hours in five pints of strong beef broth; then strain off the soup, and press as much of it as possible from the pheasants. Let it cool; and in the meantime strip the skins from the breasts, mince them small and pound them to the finest paste, with half as much fresh butter, and half of dry crumbs of bread; season these well with cayenne, sufficiently with salt, and moderately with pounded mace and grated nutmeg, and add, when their flavour is liked, three or four eschalots previously boiled tender in a little of the soup, left till cold, and minced before they are put into the mortar. Moisten the mixture with the yolks of two or three eggs, roll it into small balls of equal size, dust a little flour upon them, skim all the fat from the soup, heat it in a clean stewpan, and when it boils throw them in and poach them from ten to twelve minutes, but first ascertain that the soup is properly seasoned with salt and cayenne. We have recommended that the birds should be partially roasted before they are put into the soup-pot, because their flavour is much finer when this is done than when they are simply stewed; they should be placed rather near to a brisk fire that they may be quickly browned on the surface without losing any of their juices, and the basting should be constant. A slight thickening of rice-flour and arrow-root can be added to the soup at pleasure, and the forecemeat-balls may be fried and dropped into the tureen when they are preferred so. Half a dozen eschalots lightly browned in butter, and a small head of celery, may also be thrown in after the birds begin to stew, but nothing should be allowed to prevail over the natural flavour of the game itself; and this should be observed equally with other kinds, as partridges, grouse and venison.

Pheasants, 2: roasted 20 to 25 minutes. Strong beef broth, or stock, 5 pints: 2 to 3 hours. Forcemeat balls: breasts of pheasants, half as much dry breadcrumbs and of butter, salt, mace, cayenne; yolks of two or three eggs (and at choice 3 or 4 boiled eschalots).

Obs. The stock may be made of six pounds of shin of beef, and four quarts of water reduced to within a pint or half. An onion, a large carrot, a bunch of savoury herbs, and some salt and spice should be added to it: one pound of neck of veal or of beef will improve it.

PARTRIDGE SOUP

This is, we think, superior in flavour to the pheasant soup. It should be made in precisely the same manner, but three birds allowed for it instead of two. Grouse and partridges together will make a still finer one; the remains of roast grouse even, added to a brace of partridges, will produce a very good effect.

Eliza Acton, *Modern Cookery for Private Families*, 1845

HARE SOUP

. . . with the hare the blood is not only the life, but the flavour. That is a fact thoroughly understood by the Scotch, who imported not only their cookery from France, but the names of their favourite *plats*, and of the very crockery ware they are served on. English hare-soup is a colourless composition, whether it be clear or the less digestible *purée*. Scotch hare-soup is as much a national boast as haggis or cock-a-leekie.

A. I. Shand, *Shooting*, 1902

SCOTCH HARE SOUP

Skin and clean the hare thoroughly, saving the blood. Cut a dozen or more of very small chops from the back, shoulders and rump. Put what remains of the hare and the bones into a pot, with four pounds of fresh shin or neck of beef, four quarts of water, a couple of turnips, two carrots, six middle-sized onions, a half ounce of black and Jamaica peppercorns, an ounce of salt, a fagot of sweet herbs, and a large head of celery. Boil for three hours and strain. Brown the small chops nicely in a sauté-pan, and add them to the strained stock, and simmer for an hour and a half. Strain the blood; rub it with flour, rice-flour, or arrowroot, and a half pint of the soup, as if making starch; add more hot soup, and put the whole into the soup, which must be kept only at the point of boiling for ten minutes, lest the blood curdles. The soup may be further thickened with the parboiled liver, pounded in a mortar with the pieces of hare boiled for stock. When enough done, skim, put in a glass of catsup, and one or more of red wine, what more salt, pepper and cayenne is required, and also essence of celery. Serve with the hare-steaks in the tureen. *Obs.* Red wine, in the proportion of a quarter-pint to a tureen of soup, is reckoned an improvement by some gourmands; and those of the old school still like a large spoonful of currant-jelly dissolved in the soup.

Margaret Dods, *The Cook & Housewife's Manual*, 1870 edition

Mulligatawny Soup Made with Rabbit

For nothing does the rabbit come in more usefully than for mulligatawny: when that soup is most in request in cool weather, the rabbit is in his best condition . . .

Break up sundry rabbits and boil in three quarts of water with a quarter-ounce of black pepper. Be sure to add a slice or two of bacon. Skim the stock when it boils, and let it simmer for an hour and a half before straining. Fry some of the choice morsels of the rabbit with sliced onions in a stewpan; add the strained stock, skim, and, when it has simmered for three-quarters of an hour, throw in two dessertspoonfuls of curry powder, the same quantity of lightly browned flour, with salt and cayenne, and let it simmer again till the meat is thoroughly tender. A clove or two of garlic, shred and fried in butter, with a dash of lemon to taste, are decided improvements.

N.B. Half the secret and charm of good mulligatawny is in the successful boiling of the rice, which ought to fall light and white and dry, like snow flakes in frost or manna in the wilderness. The rice after boiling should be drained and dried before the fire in a sieve reversed.

A. I. Shand, *The Cookery of the Rabbit*, 1898

Pigeon Soup

Clean and quarter three pairs of young pigeons, and put them in milk and water and a little salt; take two pounds of the hough of beef, and the giblets of the pigeons, put them in a stew-pan with cold water, add a little salt, let them boil for two hours, and pour through a sieve. When this stock is quite cold, skim the fat clean off, return it to the stew-pan, add the pigeons, along with a handful of parsley and two onions previously minced, and boil for three-quarters of an hour. Mix with a breakfast-cupful of cream two tablespoonfuls of flour, add to the soup, and let it boil for fifteen minutes; season with pepper and salt to taste.

D. Williamson, *The Practice of Cookery & Pastry Adapted to the Business of Every-Day Life*, 1884

———————————— FISH BOUILLON ————————————

This is a clear fish soup for which any fish can be used. You want about one pound of it, also a few shrimps or mussels, to make enough soup for four people.

Melt a small piece of butter in a saucepan and fry in this for two or three minutes one leek, one carrot, one onion, two tomatoes, a piece of celery, all cut in pieces. Add a bouquet, a good pinch of mixed spice, the fish cut in pieces, boiling water, allowing for reduction—say, five and a half bowls of water, which at the end will make four—salt and pepper. Bring to the boil and simmer for at least three-quarters of an hour.

Meanwhile cut some thin slices of French roll, butter them, and spread over a mixture of grated cheese and saffron. Put these to dry and brown in the oven. Allow two or three for each person. Strain the soup before serving, and serve with it, separately, the croûtons to be put into the plates after the soup has been served.

Elvia & Maurice Firuski (eds), *The Best of Boulestin*, 1952

———————————— SALMON SOUP ————————————

The trimmings and a small slice of fresh salmon, the bones of one or two fresh whiting, carrot, turnip, onion, celery, parsley, brown breadcrumbs, potato-flour or mashed potato, water.

Put into your fish kettle the head, bones, fins and skin of the salmon, along with the bones of the whiting (these make all the difference) and the prepared vegetables—a small carrot, a small turnip, a small onion and a stick of celery. Cover amply with cold water, bring to the boil, add salt, and boil gently for at least an hour. Strain and remove all the fat and oil. Thicken with a little potato-flour or cooked and mashed potato. Add some scallops of uncooked salmon, a tablespoonful of chopped parsley and some brown breadcrumbs. As soon as the salmon is cooked, the soup is ready.

F. Marian McNeill, *The Scots Kitchen*, 1929

POTAGE OUKA

With two pounds of a fish like salmon . . . and the same amount of fish bones and trimmings, adding a large bouquet of parsley stalks, celery and fennel and salt, and moistening with five pints of water, three-quarters of a pint of white wine, make some fish stock. Cut in fine julienne strips six ounces of the white of leeks, the same of celery and two ounces of parsley roots. Stew these in butter, and finish cooking them with a little fish stock.

Clarify the fish stock with chopped whiting flesh (about a pound and a quarter) and five ounces of caviar. [A lesser quantity of lumpfish roe is an economical substitute.] Pass through a cloth. Mix the julienne with the stock, and add also dice of the fish used in making the stock.

Ambrose Heath, *Madame Prunier's Fish Cookery Book*, 1938

HAMBURG EEL SOUP

Ingredients. 1½ lbs of eel, 2½ lbs lean beef, 1 lb of pears, 1 onion, 2 carrots, 2 turnips, ½ lb of sorrel, a little sage, tarragon, thyme, 1 cup of green peas, half a cauliflower, 2 yolks of egg, white wine, salt and pepper.

Method. Skin and bone the eel, cut it in 2 to 3 inch lengths, sprinkle with salt and let it stand for 2 hours. Cut the beef to small pieces, put it in a saucepan and cover with two and a half quarts of water, bring to the boil and skim. Now add the sliced carrots, turnips, sorrel, the herbs, salt and pepper and simmer for one and a half to two hours. Add 1 cupful of peas, and the cauliflower divided into clusters. Boil till the peas and cauliflower are tender. Put the eel in a saucepan, cover with cold water, a little vinegar, add 1 sliced lemon, herbs, salt and pepper and bring to the boil. Simmer for 15 minutes till the eel is tender. Remove the pieces of eel, strain the fish stock into the meat stock, and simmer for another 15 minutes. Just before serving, add the yolks of 2 eggs, diluted with a little warm stock, and also the pears which should have been peeled, cored and quartered, and cooked in white wine, with a strip of lemon peel, till soft.

Fish Soup (Russian)

In Russia this soup is usually made from fish which are either not found in England—such as sturgeon—or which are not generally used, such as perch or tench. But it can be made with any kind of fish.

Ingredients. 3 or 4 lbs of fish, 2 quarts of water, half a glass of white wine, 2 or 3 onions, 1 stick of celery, a few spring onions, parsley, fennel, peppercorns, salt.

Method. Bone the fish and set aside about 1 lb, cut in 2 inch lengths. Put the bones and the remainder of the fish in a saucepan, cover with cold water, bring to the boil and skim. Then add the sliced vegetables, the herbs and the seasoning. Simmer gently for 1 hour. Meanwhile, cook the pieces of fish in a little butter, and either leave them whole or make into fish quenelles or dumplings. Add either the one or the other to the strained soup before serving, as well as a few spring onions, also cooked in a little butter.

Countess Morphy, *Recipes of All Nations*, c. 1930

Consolation Soup

Wash, clean and head and tail a medley of small river fish.

Fry lightly in fat some sliced potatoes, onions and as many other white vegetables as desired.

Put the fish into a saucepan with a bunch of mixed herbs, add the vegetables and enough water to cover.

Boil the fish and vegetables to a pulp, rub through a coarse sieve, and season well with salt and pepper. Reheat, and pour the soup into a deep dish, sprinkle with small crumbs of bread fried in butter, and serve very hot.

Margaret Butterworth, *Now Cook Me The Fish*, 1950

Baars (a Dutch Fish Soup)

Mrs Roundell writes of this soup as being suitable for sea or river fish. "A fresh-water Baars," she says, "can be made of small trout or gudgeons. Eels and perch can also be used."

Fillet the fish neatly in small fillets; set these aside, and put the whole of the remnants, heads, skins, bones and trimmings, into a stewpan, adding for each pound weight of such stock-stuff four ounces of onion sliced thinly, a handful of curled parsley shredded, a dessertspoonful of horseradish shavings, (a tablespoonful of parsley roots about an inch long), twelve peppercorns, a good teaspoonful of salt, a pinch of mace or mixed spice; cover with cold water, bring slowly to the boil, skim, then simmer for half an hour and strain. Into this hot broth, using another stewpan for the purpose, put the fillets of fish, with six freshly cut pieces of parsley blanched for three minutes in scalding water, and cook gently for about ten minutes until the fillets are tender. Now empty the contents of the pan into a deep dish (for the Baars is both soup and fish), and serve with thin brown bread and butter. Baars is eaten with a fork and spoon, and served in soup plates.

"Probably," Mrs Roundell adds, "the horseradish will be found sufficient without the parsley roots, and the spice may be omitted if not liked."

Ambrose Heath, *From Creel to Kitchen*, 1939

Carving and Etiquette

THE rightful importance placed on carving by our forebears has, along with other graceful accomplishments, been accorded neglect. It was the prerogative of the master of the house to carve, but few can do so now with proper skill. Present masters of the art receive a generous share of lunch and dinner invitations.

It is not very long since a weekend guest at a Scottish country house came down to breakfast early and carved himself some ham. The noble host, appearing later, was so incensed at the usurpation of his own office that the young man was sent home. Contemporary households are only too glad to welcome a carver.

On other matters of etiquette changes have been such that the customs of sixty years ago seem centuries rather than decades away. Punctuality was sacred; in the time of my maternal grandfather, Arthur Hay Drummond, if the butler failed to announce dinner at the appointed hour, even if it were a minute late and during wartime, grandfather would ostentatiously withdraw his watch from the waistcoat pocket and remark, "I can't think what has happened to dinner." That was a meal of particular formality, including dress, and improper attire was remarked on. The wearing of a tartan by someone who, in his view, was not entitled to it, elicited acid sarcasm.

Most of us would regard the rigid manners of that era as irksome, and modern informality refreshing. Yet it is regrettable that etiquette has very little place in life today, and a pity that more children are not brought up to follow the precepts set out in Robert Louis Stevenson's *A Child's Garden of Verses*:

> A child should always say what's true
> And speak when he is spoken to,

And behave mannerly at table:
At least as far as he is able.

Some Medieval Carving Terms

To break a deer
To Lyste a salmon
To unbrace a mallard
To unlace a coney
To alay a pheasant
To winge a partridge
To winge a quail
To mince a plover
To thigh a pigeon
To border a pasty
To thigh a woodcock
To splat a pike
To culpon a trout
To Trassene an eel

Carving

Such was the pointed Attention to the Minutiae of the Table that a *Boke of Kervinge* was printed, which proves that the pleasures of good Eating must have been highly valued. Carving, indeed, was, in the Feudal Times, an Art in which the superior Ranks of Men were instructed. Before a person could receive the Honour of Knighthood, it was necessary for him to fill several subordinate stations: among the rest, part of the Noviciate was passed as a Carving Esquire.

The Rev. W. B. Daniel, Rural Sports, 1807

The Art of Carving

Lord Chesterfield, touching upon this subject in one of his letters, writes: "To do the honours of the table gracefully is one of the outlines of a well-bred man; and to carve well, little as it may seem, is useful twice every day, and the doing of which ill is not only troublesome to ourselves, but renders us disagreeable and ridiculous to others." From a standpoint on a lower plane another factor presents itself, namely, economy. Pater familias, house-wives and others who follow the time-honoured custom of carving at the table seldom take the trouble to learn to carve even passably. They may manage to cut up a simple joint more or less creditably, but in carving birds their lack of skill becomes evident, and often tends to deprive them of that cool judgement and dexterity upon which so much depends, and the helpings are not only badly carved, but disproportionate and wasteful.

C. Herman Senn, *The Art of the Table*, 1923

Rules To Be Observed At City Feasts

If a clergyman happens to be at table, you are not to begin cutting up, till he has acknowledged the favour of having plenty laid before you; for though butcher and poulterer may be paid, yet something is due to Him that made butchers, poulterers, and yourselves. If no clergyman is present, somebody should be desired to officiate in his place. —Be not too eager in having the first cut, because it is ten to one but there is somebody at table more deserving. —Do not heap above two pounds of victuals upon your plate at first starting; because if you should want a further supply, the company will not fail to say, behind your back, that you are a glutton, especially if there happens to be venison, in which case everyone ought to have an equal share of the fat. —Do not drag the leg of a fowl through your teeth, in order to secure your property in it, then lay it by to pick it at your leisure. Remember also, that, though fingers were made before forks and knives, the latter were substituted in the room of the former, for the sake of cleanliness as well as carving. —If you happen to be very fond of green pease, cauliflowers, etc. recollect that some of the company may like them also. Take as little snuff as possible during your meal. —Drink not with your mouth full of victuals, because few people like them at second hand. —If puddings and tarts are served up, remember they are not brought for you alone. —Do not throw scraps off your plate into the dish, because it is possible some of the company may like cleanliness. Do not take such large

mouthfuls as to occasion your spitting part of it into your neighbour's face.—Do not throw your bones to the dog; for though it
may conceal the quantity you have eaten, the animal may
unluckily mistake your neighbour's leg for a bone of mutton;
besides, they are a sort of perquisite belonging to the dog of the
house, who is above taking any other kind of vales.—The
command, after dinner, of filling your glasses for a toast, affords an
excellent hint for eating. Suppose a person was appointed to cry
out at proper times, *load your fork*; this would prevent some men
from bolting down two or three pounds, whilst the slow eater
cannot master as many ounces. This custom once introduced,
might be easily improved, and men at a feast might be taught to
eat with as much regularity as Prussians observe in military
exercise.

The Sporting Magazine, January 1817

Serving and Carving Venison

Serving the venison is a matter of no little consequence, for the fat
has the unfortunate defect of congealing with extraordinary
celerity.

. . . Carving is to the full as important as serving . . . Meg
Dods . . . suggests mapping out a chart with cloves for the
guidance of the inexperienced. Incisions should be made longitudinally and crossways, the slices should be somewhat thin and
cut lengthways, the more delicate lying to the left, when the joint
is turned endways to the carver. But carving the haunch was
always an embarrassing piece of business, and likely to breed envy
and malice. The carver, in an excess of the charity which begins
at home, was suspected of looking after himself, of making
invidious reservations and smuggling away choice morsels.

A. I. Shand, *The Cookery of Venison*, 1896

Hare

The hare is rather difficult to manage nicely, especially if it is an
old one. When the carver has a strong wrist, the most advan-
tageous way is to carry the knife along on each side of the backbone, all the way from the shoulder to the tail, and leaving a

useless piece of back in the middle about half an inch wide, with a good fleshy fillet on each side, and the legs ready for subdivision. After this primary division, the side-slices are readily served in separate portions by cutting them across. In default of this strong-armed method, some carvers cut fillets off the back, and serve them, proceeding to do the same with the legs, which may or may not be previously raised out of their sockets. A third plan consists in removing the legs, and serving them in two portions each, then dividing the back into sections of about two or three inches in length, and finally removing the shoulders, and serving them also. If this plan is preferred, and the hare is to be carved by a person deficient in strength of wrist, the prominent part of the back-bone should be removed by the cook from the inside before roasting. The back is considered the best, then the legs, and last the shoulders, which, however, some people prefer to any other part.

PARTRIDGE AND GROUSE

The partridge is so small that it will scarcely admit of disjointing, and it is usual to separate at once into the breast portion and the back and legs, which may readily be done without cutting, by inserting the fork in the former, and raising it while depressing the latter. When this is done the knife may be carried longitudinally through the breast, so as to divide it into two equal portions, after which the back and legs may be halved in the same way. Some people, however, divide the partridge differently, by cutting off a leg and a wing together, and leaving a small breast, so as to make either three or five portions out of this bird. The grouse is carved in the same way as the partridge.

J. H. Walsh, F.R.C.S., *The British Cookery Book*, 1864

PARTRIDGE

There are several ways of carving this bird. The usual method is to carry the knife sharply along the top of the breast-bone and cut it quite through, thus dividing the bird into two equal parts. The legs and wings may be easily severed from the body . . . while the breast, if removed intact, will provide a third helping. Another easy and expeditious way of carving birds of this description is to cut them through the bones lengthwise and across, thus forming four portions.

Mrs Beeton, *All-About Cookery*, c. 1930

──────────── PHEASANT ────────────

A pheasant may be sliced on the breast like a turkey, after which, if the party require it, the plan of carving similar to that practised on roast fowl must be adopted.

J. H. Walsh, F.R.C.S., *The British Cookery Book*, 1864

──────────── PHEASANT ────────────

Fix the fork in the breast, and cut slices from neck to tail. If more helpings are wanted, take off the legs and wings, as in carving a fowl, and be careful in taking off the wing to hit the exact point between it and the neck-bone. Next cut off the merrythought, and then divide the other parts exactly as a fowl. The prime bits are the same as in a fowl. The brains are fancied.

Margaret Dods, *The Cook & Housewife's Manual*, 1870 edition

──────────── WILD DUCK ────────────

The breasts of wild-fowl are the only parts of them held in much estimation, and these are carved in slices from the legs to the neck.

Eliza Acton, *Modern Cookery for Private Families*, 1845

─────── TO UNBRACE A MALLARD OR DUCK ───────

First, raise the pinions and legs, but cut them not off; then raise the merry-thought (wishbone) from the breast, and lace it down both sides with your knife.

Hannah Glasse, *The Art of Cookery Made Plain & Easy*, 1796

---------- WOODCOCK ----------

This bird, like a partridge, may be carved by cutting it exactly into two similar portions, or made into three helpings, as described in carving partridge. The backbone is considered the tit-bit of a woodcock, and by many the thigh is also thought a great delicacy.

---------- SNIPE ----------

One of these small but delicious birds may be given whole to a gentleman; but in helping a lady it will be better to cut them quite through the centre, completely dividing them into equal and like portions.

---------- THE CARVING OF FISH ----------

A steel knife and fork should never be used for fish because contact with this metal is apt to spoil its flavour. A silver or plated slice and fork should be provided for carving and serving it. When serving fish be careful not to break the flakes. Short-grained fish, such as salmon, should be cut lengthwise.

Mrs Beeton, *All-About Cookery*, c. 1930

ON KEEPING BUTCHER'S MEAT, GAME, ETC.

The following are a few hints . . . out of a little volume lately published, entitled *The Experienced Butcher*, which, to housekeepers and heads of families, contains more useful and profitable suggestions than the title seems to imply:

Charcoal powder is a very powerful antiseptic, and meat may be preserved, or rendered much more palatable, even when considerably tainted, by covering it with charcoal powder, or by burying it for a few hours underground: this is probably owing to the carbon, or charcoal, contained in the earth.

Meat, and even game, may be preserved, by wrapping it in a clean linen cloth and burying it in a box filled with dry sand, where it will remain sweet for three weeks, if deposited in an airy, dry, and cool chamber. A joint of meat is frequently kept for some time in the tub, box, or heap of salt, belonging to a grocer, being merely put in well covered with salt.

Veal and lamb (and indeed other meats) are preserved in Germany by immersing them in skimmed milk, so as to cover the whole joint. In warm weather, the milk should be changed twice the first day, and once in twenty-four hours afterwards: but, in a cool temperature, it is sufficient to renew it every two or three days. Thus the meat may be kept in a sweet state for several weeks; but it ought to be washed in spring water before it is dressed.

A joint of meat may be preserved for several days, even in summer, by wrapping it in a clean linen cloth, previously moistened with good vinegar, placing it in an earthen pan, or hanging it up, and changing the cloth, or wringing it out afresh in vinegar, once or twice a day, if the weather be very warm.

The following method of destroying the smell and effects of putrid meat is given in Flindall's "Complete Family Assistant": Put the meat, if intended for making soup, into a saucepan of water, scum it when it boils, and then throw into the saucepan a burning coal, very compact, and free from smoak. Leave it there for two or three minutes, and it will have contracted all the smell of the meat and the soup. If the meat is to be roasted, put it first into the water till it boils, and, after having scummed it, throw a burning coal into the boiling water, as before. At the end of two minutes, take out the meat, and having wiped it well, in order to dry it, put it upon the spit.

The Sporting Magazine, August 1817

Venison

I DO not suppose that many housewives will be eager to follow the instructions "saw up stag's head and remove brains". But at least the several writers I have quoted, Margaret Fraser particularly, indicate the versatility of venison, the whole animal being worthy of use. I have borrowed extensively from Mrs Fraser for one simple reason: not only was she a professional cook, but she was also the wife of the head stalker at Lochluichart. Her unique experience is reflected in her common-sense recipes.

Few people nowadays have the services of a Mrs Fraser to perform the esoteric tasks she describes. But those who are adventurous enough to want to sample the more arcane parts of the animal, will probably find that if they have a butcher who stocks venison he will be glad to prepare those pieces which would otherwise be sold as dog food. Offal is unpopular, cheap, delicious and deserves higher recognition.

While venison that the urban shopper can buy nowadays in super-markets is very different from the meat of the purely wild animal, as a product of farmed deer it is comparable to the venison from deer kept in parks from time immemorial, and which was the principal meat eaten by our early forebears. In both cases the beasts are artificially fed and are killed young. The traditional venison of the wild animal, be it fallow from the English forest or red deer of the Scottish hills, is very different. A sportsman will not ordinarily cull a beast until it is in its prime, and it may therefore be as much as ten years old. Such meat is very strong and tough and needs long and slow cooking. It will also need time in marinade to make it tender. Do not make the mistake, however, of marinading young meat, for what is gained in tenderness is lost in flavour.

Much pleasure in food has been lost in the craze for youth and tenderness. The latter should be sought, but flavour is often sacrificed in that search. Five-year-old wether (castrated male) mutton was formerly regarded as the prime meat from sheep, but now it would be uneconomic to produce and the public are ignorant of its superiority to lamb. My wife, who breeds Jacob sheep, kills her lambs at not less than a year old. Our guests, even if not told of the age of these "lambs", which by definition should not be more than six months old, comment on their exceptional flavour.

As with undue caution on tenderness, so can there be too much regard for leanness. Wild deer that have lived well may have layers of exterior fat. As it is cooked the flavour of the meat will be improved by that fat. The flesh of deer from farm or park, though ostensibly free from fat will, because of the idle life the animal has led in contrast to the wild kinsman, be suffused with fat that is not readily visible. Fatness and leanness can be misleading terms.

Disagreement has always existed on the subjective question of what is the best species of deer for the table. Fallow and red have always had a favoured following, but roe has its detractors. When roe deer habitat consists of coniferous plantations, with little access to open grassland, then it can acquire the unpleasant taste of turpentine. But more often than not, the meat is finer in texture and flavour than the other species.

For those fortunate enough to have a deer in their larder, it should be hung for up to a fortnight. The time must, obviously, depend on weather conditions, but do not worry if the surface of the flesh turns a blue-black colour. While the carcase is hanging we insert an orange into the rib cavity. This is stuck with cocktail sticks upon which are impaled cloves and bay leaves. A particular sweetness is thus imparted. Sweetness, it must be emphasised, is never an attribute of stags or bucks, or any other male animal, in rut. Once they start consorting with females the flesh becomes coarse and rank and is to be avoided.

Finally, on the preparation of liver, I believe I can improve on Margaret Fraser's suggestion that it should be kept for two days. Our household has a tradition, not altogether popular, that the liver be brought fresh to the breakfast table. In that state it is, for most people, too strong. The remedy is to steep it in milk for twenty-four hours.

The Civic Haunch

We dare to say that the typical haunch, with all that precedes and follows it, from the iced punch and Madeira to the curious old cognac, has done more than the example of Whittington or Gresham to animate aspirants to the gown and the golden chain.

An Uninvited Guest

. . . It was Theodore Hook who, strolling through Mayfair with Terry, the protégé of Walter Scott, was arrested by . . .

> Ketchin' smells of roast and boiled
> A' coming from the kitchen.

. . . He looked down and saw his favourite joint. He did not know the gentleman who owned it from Adam, but again he walked in, presented his friend, procured an invitation, enjoyed an excellent dinner; was, of course, the life and soul of the society, and won the gratitude of the good gentleman he had victimised by making the evening go off delightfully. So much so that he could afford to close his brilliant improvisations on the piano with the confession,

> I'm very much pleased with your fare,
> Your cellar's as prime as your cook,
> My friend's Mr Terry the player,
> And I'm Mr Theodore Hook.

A. I. Shand, *Cookery of Venison*, 1896

The Best Venison

. . . there is no food on the hill . . . that deer are so fond of as the tender tops of young heather or newly-burnt ground . . . high ground in summer gives the sweetest pickings, and stags that dwell habitually among the stony tops make incomparably the best venison.

A. G. Cameron, *The Wild Red Deer of Scotland*, 1923

The Best Venison

Young deer are worthless for the table, though in the sub-tropics I have eaten savoury dishes of fawn which were most excellently tender. So much depends on condition, sex, age, and the recent feeding of deer that it is difficult to lay down any particular canon of excellence. The haunch of a hart of grease may be equalled or even surpassed by that of a yeld hind, or the cutlets of an undistinguished young stag may be far better than the civet of a monarch of the forest.

In some forests, and more particularly among herds of fallow deer in parks, a proportion of the young male fawns are emasculated. This operation produces a steer or dehorned stag whose venison is far less coarse in flavour, but which, like all venison, tends to lack adequate fat. Buck venison contains far more fat than deer, and the roe is leanest of all; But whereas red deer venison should be selected largely for that which has the most fat, this is no safe index for park deer, which may have been stall-fed for the market and whose meat is fat but coarse.

H. B. C. Pollard, *The Sportsman's Cookery Book*, 1926

Roe Venison

The flesh of the roe buck is the most wholesome to eat of any other wild beast's flesh; they live on good herbs and other woods and vines and on briars and hawthorns with leaves and on all growth of young trees.

Edward, Second Duke of York, *The Master of Game*, c. 1410

Roe Venison

The roe is out of season the greater part of the year. Roe are sometimes in pride of grease, and when shot in this state are superior venison to either red or fallow deer. When a roe is out of condition, stewing and larding may disguise it as food, just as the French cook, by the help of condiments, made his master eat his old slippers; but people who would so treat a roe-haunch in prime order deserve never to have an opportunity of spoiling one again. The haunches of all our prime roes are simply roasted, and I never

saw any one partake of them who did not say they were the most
delicate and delicious of venison.

John Colquhoun, *The Moor and the Loch*, 1888 edition

Sending Away

Haunches should be kept a few days before being sent away so that
the fat becomes well set, and the date of the kill should be on the
label.

Augustus Grimble, *More Leaves from My Game Book*, 1917

Preparations in the Larder

When the deer has been transferred to the larder it must be closely
attended to. If the pipe running along the backbone is not cut out
the flesh will taint, and the mould which will gather on the meat
must be wiped off from time to time. It should be dusted at
intervals with flour and pepper, and when the haunch is to be
cooked, it should be sponged with warm water and rubbed
industriously with lard. Then it is to be covered with sheets of
paper steeped in butter or salad oil, and swathed in a thick paste of
flour and water.

A. I. Shand, *Shooting*, 1902

Hanging

Venison is by nature a strong-scented meat and can be hung from
two to three weeks before getting into condition. Owing, perhaps, to its strong odour, venison is all too often condemned as
having gone too far before it is really ripe at all. Personally I do not
like my meat in the state of advanced corruption affected by many
epicures, but venison must either be hung or lengthily marinaded
in order to get it properly tender.

The beast should be bled and "grallocked"—i.e., drawn the
moment he is killed . . . The joints when skinned should be
rubbed down with flour plentifully mixed with powdered ginger
and pepper. This dressing helps as a surface preservative and
discourages the disgusting blow-fly. Venison hung in a larder

should be masked in butter muslin, but should be taken down and inspected every day and the pepper dressing renewed if necessary. The loin or saddle is rather more likely to taint than the haunch, and particular care should be taken to see that the furrow of the backbone is well dressed with pepper. Cut away any unnecessary portions or anything like a shot wound, which will taint readily.

In general venison should hang at least a week before it is fit to cook. A gift of venison which has arrived in doubtful condition should be washed in warm water, which will remove any surface taint, and then if it is found to be sound and it is not convenient to cook it for a day or two it should be floured and peppered and hung up, or laid on a dish, with a few pieces of charcoal that have been heated in the oven. Burnt bread in a bag makes an excellent substitute. This use of charcoal as a deodorant is to be recommended where venison has to be hung in a small larder. Sponging over with a solution of the disinfectant known as Milton, which is non-poisonous, is also an excellent way of purifying venison.

General Preparation

In hot weather it is better to carve a saddle or neck into cutlets and marinade them in the Marinade No. 3 given for hare [page 99] than to hang. The same applies to warm countries where it is difficult to keep meat till tender; meat kept in a marinade will keep far longer and not taint at all provided it is turned or basted occasionally.

The cookery of venison is limited mainly to the roast and braise; soup is sometimes made, and venison also makes savoury hashes and remade dishes. Its virtue is largely resident in a careful preparation of the gravy and concomitant sauces, and, above all, venison needs to be served on remarkably hot plates and kept on a really hot dish, for its fat congeals quicker than any other, and the sauces will thicken and set at the slightest chill.

H. B. C. Pollard, *The Sportsman's Cookery Book*, 1926

Serving

Serving the venison is a matter of no little consequence, for the fat
has the unfortunate defect of congealing with extraordinary
celerity. As a rule, eating off gold or silver plate is one of the
penalties of ostentatious magnificence, with which the gourmand
would willingly dispense. There must always be an unpleasant
assiete-pensée of plate-powder lurking in the chasings and stray
corners. But with venison, in a small and select company, silver,
or the humbler pewter, with spirit lamps beneath, may be used
with great advantage. Always sensitive to the fleeting nature of
earthly pleasures, the bitter lesson is never more forcibly brought
home to the epicure than when the venison fat and gravy are
congealing visibly on china before his eyes. The evanescent joy
eludes him unless he bolt the delicacies American fashion, which
is fatal to his hopes, obnoxious to his principles, and attended by
indigestion, dyspepsia and remorse.

Wine

We have said our say elsewhere against the practice of mixing
wines at dinner, and serving various vintages, however rich and
rare, with the several courses. We said it was a sound rule to stick
to champagne, nor have we anything to retract. But no rule is
without its exceptions, and we are bound to admit an exception in
the case of venison. For with venison Burgundy goes as naturally
as iced punch with the turtle and with far more obvious reason.
The bouquet of the one and the savour of the other were evidently
predestined to make a happy love-match.

A. I. Shand, *The Cookery of Venison*, 1896

Roast Haunch

Take down the haunch and wash it well in hot water to remove the
dressing. Trim off the knuckle; dry and rub the surface well with butter.
Now cover the whole surface with sheets of paper that have been
thoroughly dipped in salad oil and bind them tight with oiled twine.
Roast for two and a half to three hours, basting with butter and

turning frequently. Half an hour before it is cooked remove the paper and let it brown nicely.

Make a thick gravy out of the trimmings of venison cooked in stock, and add to this a double glass of port and a glass of red currant jelly. A teaspoonful of spiced sugar made by pounding up an inch-long roll of cinnamon bark and a clove with pieces of lump sugar is a valuable addition.

——————— Fried Venison Cutlets ———————

Season, flour and dip in run butter. Egg and breadcrumb them thickly, or give a double coating by dipping in run butter and again in egg and breadcrumb once the first cover has "set". Fry in deep hot lard or oil for ten minutes. Serve with an Espagnole, Tartare or Piquante Sauce.

H. B. C. Pollard, *The Sportsman's Cookery Book*, 1926

——————— To Roast Red Deer or Roe ———————

Season the haunch highly, by rubbing it well with mixed spices. Salt it for six hours in claret and a quarter pint of the best vinegar, or the fresh juice of three lemons; turn it frequently, and baste with the liquor. Strain the liquor in which the venison was soaked; add to it fresh butter melted, and with this baste the haunch during the whole time it is roasting. Fifteen minutes before the roast is drawn, remove the paper, and froth and brown it as directed in other receipts. For *sauce*—Take the contents of the dripping-pan, which will be very rich and highly flavoured: add a half-pint of clear brown gravy, drawn from venison or full-aged heath mutton. Boil them up together; skim, add a teaspoonful of walnut-catsup, lemon juice or any of the flavoured vinegars most congenial to venison, and to the taste of the gastronome may advantageously be substituted. After the third venison dinner, it was the recorded opinion of the Club, that it is downright idiocy and a wanton and profligate sacrifice of the palate and the stomach to the vanity of the eye, to roast venison when it is not *fat*, while so many more nutritious and palatable modes of cookery may be employed, in collops, soup, pasty or civet.

Margaret Dods, *The Cook & Housewife's Manual*, 1870 edition

—————— VENISON CUTLETS WITH CHESTNUT PURÉE ——————

Four to six venison cutlets, one and a half ounces of butter, one egg, breadcrumbs, chestnut purée, half-glaze sauce and seasoning.

Pare the cutlets neatly, flatten and trim again; season them with pepper and salt; beat up the egg; dip each cutlet in egg and cover with breadcrumbs. Melt the butter in a sauté pan; when hot, put in the cutlets and fry each side a nice brown colour; take up, drain and dish up in a circle on a small bed of mashed potatoes. Fill the centre with chestnut purée; pour a little demi-glaze or other thin brown sauce round the base of the dish, and serve.

Chestnut purée is made as follows: Boil a pound of large chestnuts for twenty minutes; remove shell and pell [the brown pith]; boil again in a little stock and when quite tender rub through a fine wire sieve. Season with salt and pepper and moisten with a very little brown sauce, tomato sauce or rich stock.

Georgiana, Countess of Dudley, *A Second Dudley Book of Cookery*, 1914

—————————————— VENISON STEW ——————————————

The shoulder is often too lean to roast, and is generally somewhat dry. But with simple treatment and small expenditure in spices—which in this case may be judiciously used in moderation—it makes an admirable stew, and, as Mr Micawber remarked of the devil of underdone mutton, there are few better comestibles in its way. Keep the shoulder till it bones easily. Flatten and cover with slices of fat mutton. Sprinkle with spices and roll it up. Stew in a close pan in beef or mutton gravy, and when nearly ready for dishing, add some wine, or, if strict economy be a consideration, we suggest that ale may serve.

A. I. Shand, *The Cookery of Venison*, 1896

—————————————— VENISON IRISH STEW ——————————————

Take a piece of ribs of venison. Soak in salt and water for 1 hour till blanched, cut into squares and cook for 2 hours in sufficient water to cover it. Put away till cold, when remove all fat. Add a few pieces of carrot, turnip and onion, and boil for ½ hour. Next add raw potatoes (peeled) and boil till potatoes are cooked.

Venison Pudding

Take ½ lb of clean venison suet. Chop finely and make into a paste by adding ¾ lb flour, pinch of salt and cold water. Line a bowl with this paste. Cut some venison into small cubes and also a kidney if available. Season with pepper, salt and chopped onion and fill up the bowl, adding some cold water. Cover with a layer of paste and steam for 4 hours. When ready, fill up with boiling stock.

Venison Curry

Cut about 2 to 3 lb lean venison (from haunch) into cubes. Season with pepper and salt. Fry up 1 large onion, 1 apple, and tomato, and then add venison, along with 1 dessertspoonful curry powder and ½ teaspoonful ginger. Cook slowly for 2 to 3 hours with lid on pan, stirring occasionally and adding a spoonful of stock if required.

Ten minutes before serving, stir in a tablespoonful Indian chutney and a pinch of sugar. Serve with boiled rice.

Margaret Fraser, A Highland Cookery Book, 1930

Braised Haunch

Trim a small haunch vigorously and put it in a casserole or braising-pan with two sliced onions, three sliced carrots, two cups of chopped celery, thyme, parsley, peppercorns, bay-leaves, three cloves, and a blade of mace. Add half a bottle of good claret and as much stock. Close the casserole tight with buttered paper between lid and joint, and bring it to the boil; then allow to cook in a moderate oven for three hours, basting with the juice from time to time.

When done change the joint over to a buttered baking-pan and add a portion of the juice to the braise. Brush the surface of the joint with glaze to colour, strain the remainder of the sauce, and add a glass of port and a saltspoonful of cayenne pepper. Thicken by reducing, and pour over the joint before serving.

——————————— Roast Saddle of Venison ———————————

Skin and trim, cover with strips of bacon, and bind round with string.
Lay a rasher or two of fat bacon and a layer of sliced carrots and onions
in a baking-tin, add an ounce of butter and seasoning. Roast in a hot
oven for a quarter of an hour, then reduce heat, and continue to roast
slowly for another two hours at least. Skim the gravy of fat and set aside
a portion of it to make the usual sauce (as with roast haunch): pour the
rest round the joint on the dish. Some people baste with port wine or
claret added to the dish gravy before the joint is withdrawn from the
oven.

H. B. C. Pollard, *The Sportsman's Cookery Book*, 1926

——————————— Fillets of Venison Sautéed ———————————

Cut some thin slices from a piece of venison which has not been
marinated, and put them in a fireproof china dish. Put in a saucepan a
glass of wine vinegar, a bay leaf, a sprig of thyme, one onion with a
clove, one chopped shallot, parsley and a small piece of cinnamon.
Bring to the boil and cook five minutes. Pass through a fine strainer, let
it get cold and pour this marinade over the slices of venison. Let this
stand one hour in a cool place.

Melt some butter in a sauteuse, cook the fillets (they should not be
too well cooked) and put them in the serving dish. Add to the butter in
the sauteuse a glass of brandy, the marinade, a little consommé or stock
and a small piece of butter worked in with flour; reduce for a few
minutes, whip well, pour over the fillets, and cook a little more.

If you want to have a garniture with it, you can serve either purée of
chestnuts and red currant jelly or, more subtly, slices of eating apples
fried in butter.

Elvia and Maurice Firuski (eds), *The Best of Boulestin*, 1952

——————————— Venison Steaks ———————————

Steaks are cut from the loin end of the haunch, as this is the most
tender. They should be cut about one inch thick, leaving on them
plenty of fat. Run a little salad oil over them and grill quickly a nice
brown. The length of time they require for grilling depends upon

whether they are preferred juicy or much cooked. Place on a dish which has been made hot, and pour over them a little chopped parsley and lemon juice and season with salt and pepper.

Serve with them some fried onions (and mushrooms, if any at hand), also a little currant jelly in a boat.

───────────────── POTTED VENISON ─────────────────

Take the meat of cooked venison and pound it in a mortar until thoroughly bruised. Add one ounce of fresh butter, a few peppercorns, a grate of nutmeg, pepper and salt to taste. When well mixed and pounded, pass through a fine wire sieve and place in a small potted-meat dish. Melt a little fresh butter and run it over to cover the top. Put in a cool place until cold.

A little thick cream can be added to the potted meat, whilst being pounded, if this is liked.

───────────────── HASHED VENISON ─────────────────

Cut some thin slices, with plenty of fat, off a haunch of venison which has been cooked the previous day. Place this ready in a stewpan with cover, and prepare the following sauce:

Take two tablespoonfuls of red currant jelly, one tumbler of port wine, one tumbler of claret, three bay leaves, six black peppercorns, four cloves and one pint of good brown sauce which has been made of venison essence (the shoulder and sinewy parts serve for this). First melt the jelly, then add the wine, spice and bay leaves. Let this reduce a little, then pour in the brown sauce and allow all to simmer for about ten minutes, and strain through a tammy or muslin. This should be poured over the sliced venison, and all made very hot, but not allowed to boil.

Serve in silver dish over a lamp or hot water, with slices of venison fat cut very thin and laid on the top.

If the haunch has little or no fat, thin slices of white beef fat can be substituted.

Venison Collops

Take one pound of raw venison cut from the loin and free it from fat and sinew. Mince it and place it in a stewpan with three ounces of butter and one large onion cut in four pieces and wet with a pint of good light stock, either made from venison or any stock there may be at hand. Season well with salt and pepper and let all cook; then remove the onion.

Have ready a border of mashed potatoes, prepared with a little butter or cream and nicely browned. Pile up the collops in the centre, and serve.

The mince should be thick and firm.

Georgiana, Countess of Dudley, *A Second Dudley Book of Cookery*, 1914

To Fry Venison Collops, Scottish

Cut nice steaks from the haunch, or slices neatly trimmed from the neck or loin. Have a gravy drawn from the bones and trimmings, ready thickened with butter rolled in lightly browned flour. Strain it into a small stew-pan, boil, and add a squeeze of lemon or orange, and a small glass of claret: pepper to taste, a salt-spoonful of salt, the size of a pin's head of cayenne, and a scrape of nutmeg. Fry and dish the collops hot, and pour this sauce over them. A still higher goût may be imparted to this sauce by eschalot wine, basil wine, or tarragon vinegar, chosen as may suit the taste of the eater. If these flavours are not liked, some old venison-eaters may relish a very little pounded fine sugar and vinegar in the gravy, and currant-jelly may be served in a sauce tureen. Garnish with fried crumbs. This is an excellent way of dressing venison, particularly when it is not fat enough to roast well.

Margaret Dods, *The Cook & Housewife's Manual*, 1870 edition

Venison Pasty

Historically and gastronomically the pasty ranks next to the haunch. It is economical, too, for anything may be used for it, although the breast is generally preferred. Cut the pieces small, trimming away bone and skin. Bones and unconsidered trimmings make excellent gravy. Distribute impartially the fat and the lean; if the fat fall short, as is probable, supplement with good mutton, season with pepper etc., pour in the gravy with the indispensable additions of red wine and white vinegar; do not forget to add mushrooms, if procurable, and failing these, shred in a few onions. A squeeze of a lemon gives zest to the dish, and, as Bailie Jarvie's father, the Deacon, said of a boiled tup's head, an overdone pasty is rank poison. An hour and a half of baking in the oven should suffice for a moderate-sized dish. In any case, underdoing is a fault on the right side which can easily be rectified. N.B. In the opinion of most competent judges a pasty slightly underdone is decidedly better cold than hot.

A. I. Shand, *The Cookery of Venison*, 1896

Margaret Sim's Pasty

Margaret Sim was cook to Colquhoun of Luss, at Rossdhu on Loch Lomond.

Cut a neck or breast into small steaks, rub them over with a seasoning of parsley, shallot, and a sprig of thyme minced very fine, add grated nutmeg, pepper, and salt. Roll the pieces of venison separately in the herbs, fry them slightly in butter, line the sides and edges of a pie dish with puff-paste, place the pieces of venison in the pie dish, add about half a pint of rich gravy made from the trimmings of the venison, add half a glass of port wine and the juice of half a lemon, cover the dish with puff-paste, and bake it nearly two hours in a moderate oven; when nearly done, open it a little at the top or side and pour a little more gravy into the pie before closing it up.

Patrick R. Chalmers, *Deerstalking*, 1935

Venison Steak and Kidney Pie

Take a piece of venison and a kidney, cut each into cubes, season, and put into a pie-dish with some grated onion and parsley. Fill up with stock or water. Cover with puff pastry and bake for 3 hours, adding stock at intervals.

Venison Cakes

Take about 2 lb fleshy venison with some fat on it, ½ lb breadcrumbs, and a small onion. Pass three times through a mincing machine. Add seasoning. Shape into cakes and fry in butter.

—————   Venison Cakes Made from Cooked Meat   —————

Take any pieces of cooked venison, add a raw egg, pepper, salt and a small onion, and a large handful of breadcrumbs. Pass all two or three times through mincing machine. Shape into cakes and fry in hot fat.

These may be brushed over with egg and rolled in breadcrumbs before frying if desired.

———————————————   Venison Sausages   ———————————————

Take 1 lb venison from haunch, ½ lb ham fat, and ½ lb lean ham, ½ lb fresh bread. Put all ingredients through mincing machine twice. Add pepper and a very small pinch of salt. Mix all well together and form into sausages, patties or cutlets and fry.

Margaret Fraser, A *Highland Cookery Book*, 1930

———————————————————   Gravy   ———————————————————

Celerity in sending from the fire to the table is everything, and the brown gravy poured over the meat should be as hot as the dish on which it is served. The recipes for gravy are various, although all suggest similar ingredients. A very good one is a pound of currant jelly, a gill of port and the rind of a lemon with a flavouring of cinnamon. Other experts substitute claret for port—which we think a mistake—and suggest the addition of cloves and nutmegs, cinnamon and cayenne. These details must be matters of taste and fancy.

A. I. Shand, *The Cookery of Venison*, 1896

———————————————————   Gravy   ———————————————————

Make a pint of gravy of trimmings of venison, or shanks of mutton, thus: Broil the meat on a quick fire till it is browned, then stew it slowly. Strain, skim, and serve the gravy it yields, adding salt and a teaspoonful of walnut-pickle.

VENISON SAUCES

Venison may have a sweet, a sharp, or a savoury sauce.

Sharp Sauce. A quarter-pound of the best loaf-sugar, or white candy-sugar dissolved in a half-pint of champagne vinegar, and carefully skimmed.

Sweet Sauce. Melt some white or red currant jelly with a glass of white or red wine, whichever suits best in colour; or serve the jelly unmelted in a sauce-tureen. This last sauce answers well for hare, fawn, or kid, and to many tastes for roast mutton.

Melon-pickle. We reckon better still for either roast venison or mutton. It is made thus: Pare, seed, and slice two or three rather unripe small melons; soak them in vinegar for a week or ten days; drain off and simmer the slices in fresh vinegar till as tender as pickled beet; again drain, and leave the slices on the sieve reversed; and when dry, put them into a pickle bottle, and pour over them a thin syrup, made in the proportion of a pint of water to twelve ounces of sugar, and in which some cloves have been infused. Let them soak in the syrup for a week or more, and, pouring the half of it off them, fill up the bottles with the best vinegar, which, as for all pickles to keep, is first boiled and left to get quite cold.

Savoury Sauce. [See page 83 in her recipe to roast red deer or roe.]

Margaret Dods, *The Cook & Housewife's Manual*, 1870 edition

The Excellence of Offal

The heart is best cooked stuffed with veal stuffing and roasted. It may be eaten to the accompaniment of currant jelly. The liver must be sliced and fried. The kidneys grilled and served on toast go with a crisp rasher or so. And the delicate tongues are to be boiled and served as an entrée, or as a luncheon dish with French beans and a thick, brown gravy. Even the "monyplies", the sage-green membranes of the third digestive pouch, are capital if cleaned carefully and stewed in milk after the mode of tripe.

Patrick R. Chalmers, *Deerstalking*, 1935

STAG'S HEART STUFFED

Take a stag's heart, clean blood channels and remove all fibre. Prepare a stuffing by mincing together ¼ lb beef or venison suet, 1 small onion (grated), 1 spoonful chopped parsley, 6 oz breadcrumbs, pepper, salt, sage and any other desired flavouring. Fill up centre of heart, sew up and roast in a pan, turning frequently. Cook for about 2 hours.

STAG'S LIVER

Skin liver and cut in slices. Season with pepper and salt. Roll in flour, then brush with egg, roll in breadcrumbs and fry in butter. After it has browned nicely put cover on frying pan, draw it to side of range and let it simmer for ½ hour, turning the slices occasionally. Serve on a foundation of mashed potato, with fried bacon and brown sauce.

STAG'S KIDNEYS FRIED

Skin and remove fibre from kidneys, cut in slices, season with pepper and salt, sprinkle with flour. Fry in butter and serve on toast with gravy poured over.

STAG'S BRAINS

Saw up stag's head and remove brains. Blanch in salt and water for about 10 minutes, remove from boiling water, and drain. Sprinkle with seasoning, roll in flour and fry in butter. Serve on toast with bacon.

STAG'S HEAD PIE

Clean a stag's head well, and boil till tender. Remove all flesh from the bones, and put away to cool. Next day take the cheeks and tongue and cut them in slices. Arrange in alternate layers in a pie-dish and fill up with good strong consommé. Add seasoning, and cover with puff paste. Bake for 2 hours, occasionally adding consommé. When cooked, add a cupful of aspic jelly made from venison stock, and serve cold.

Stag's Tongue (Fresh)

Take one or more tongues and after washing well place in a pan of water with plenty of vegetables to flavour and a pinch of salt.

Boil for 3 hours. Remove skin and fibre, cut through centre, brush with egg, roll in breadcrumbs, and fry in butter. Dish in a circle on a foundation of mashed potato with vegetables heaped up in centre, and a good brown sauce poured round.

Stag's Tripe

Take the stomach bag and wash well in cold water. Then immerse it in a pan of *boiling* water. Remove from fire and cover up for 5 minutes, after which the brown coating can easily be scraped off with a knife. Wash again thoroughly, put into a pan and bring through boil in order to shrink it. Remove from pan and with a kitchen scissors cut it into small squares. Simmer these in water with 2 or 3 onions for at least 6 hours. Remove onions when cooked, chop them up, add a piece of butter and make a white sauce by adding 1 tablespoonful flour, using the stock in which the tripe was boiled to thin it down. After the sauce has boiled add 2 tablespoonfuls cream and a small teaspoonful mustard. Put the cooked tripe into this sauce and bring through the boil. Serve plain or with tomato sauce.

Scotch Haggis

Clean stomach bag as in Recipe for Tripe. Take the heart, liver, and a piece of the lights and boil these for an hour. When cold, chop the heart and lights as finely as possible, and grate the liver with a fine grater. Take of these the following quantities: ½ cupful lights, ½ cupful heart, 2 cupfuls liver, 1 cupful chopped suet (beef or venison), 1 cupful oatmeal, 2 large onions finely chopped, pepper and salt. Mix well together in their dry state, and then moisten with stock or water. Put the mixture into the stomach bag, or a part of it if the whole is too large. Sew it up, leaving plenty of space for expansion. Prick well with a skewer, and tie in a pudding cloth. Boil for 2 hours. Remove cloth, and send to table in the bag, making an incision.

The same mixture might be put into a pudding bowl, the top covered with suet paste, and boiled for 2 hours. Serve from bowl.

DEERFOOT JELLY

Take feet of 2 stags, skin and wash well, and put on with 3 quarts of water and boil slowly for 8 hours. Do not let the water reduce in boiling. Strain through soup cloth, and let it stand overnight. Next day remove all fat. Turn the jelly into a clean saucepan, add to it ¾ lb loaf sugar, juice and rind of 4 lemons, a few cloves and any other spice desired, the white and shell of 4 fresh eggs. Whisk over the fire till it boils. Draw to the side and simmer for ½ hour. Strain through a jelly bag, or through a piece of airplane fabric, when it should turn out as clear as crystal. Add sherry or any other liqueur if desired, and leave to stiffen.

STEWED KIDNEYS

Skin and remove fibre from kidneys, and fry as in other recipe.

When browned, add a sliced onion and a small quantity of stock, and putting a cover on the pan let them simmer for 2 to 3 hours. Thicken sauce with corn-flour, add a spoonful of chopped parsley and serve.

This can be varied by the addition of vegetables or tomatoes if desired.

OATMEAL OR WHITE PUDDINGS

Take 1 cupful stag's kidney suet, 1 cupful oatmeal, 1 onion (chopped), pepper and salt to taste. Mix all together and boil either tied up in a cloth, or put into skins for the purpose. These can be bought at any butcher's shop.

Margaret Fraser, A Highland Cookery Book, 1930

Suitable Wines

To drink Burgundy of the best with venison is common form. Personally I find Burgundy too rich a wine and, as an everyday beverage to match the haunch, I prefer a hock. Or, upon a gala night, two glasses of dry champagne.

Patrick R. Chalmers, Deerstalking, 1935

Hare

THROUGHOUT Europe, Asia and Africa, fable is inherent in the history of the hare. The Romans feared it, the Druids would not eat it. Forty years ago, in the neighbourhood of Ullapool in Ross & Cromarty, I was told of two women who were supposed to be witches. No one would consciously cross their paths and, among their attributes, they had allegedly been seen to change themselves into the guise of hares.

By the 14th century British prejudice against the hare as food had gone, probably dissipated by the eating habits of foreign invaders, Norman or otherwise. A hare is an ideal size for feeding a family, and the common animal is the brown hare. This is the creature of the lowland pastures and arable fields which is seven pounds or more in weight.

The epicure, however, will seek out the mountain hare, a lighter animal by a few pounds. Curiously neglected for its quality, it feeds on the natural, wild herbage of the hills and, as with hill sheep and grouse, whose principal food is heather, it has the subtle flavour that distinguishes it from animals that feed on cultivated grass and other crops. The meat of the mountain hare is much akin to that of grouse, and that is its best recommendation.

Cosmetic Quality

Pliny assures us that the flesh of hares causes sleep, and that those who are in the habit of eating them, look fair, lovely and gracious, for a week afterwards.

. . . The blood of this Animal is sweeter, and held in higher estimation than the blood of any other. It possesses several qualities, when applied warm to the skin; it not only clears it, but renders it delicately white.

R. B. Thornhill, *The Shooting Directory*, 1804

A Warning against Hare

Hare's flesh, especially if it be of an old hare, is of a very dry temper, of a hard digestion, and breedeth melancholy more than any other flesh, which the blacknesse thereof convinceth. Wherefore, it is not for the goodnesse of the meat that hares are so often hunted, but for recreation and exercising of the body; for it maketh a very dry, thick, and melancholick blood, bindeth the belly, and being often eaten, breeds incubus, and causeth fearfull dreams. The younger are far better, by reason that the natural siccity of the flesh is somewhat tempered by the moisture of tender age. The flesh of young hares is somewhat easily digested, is acceptable to the palat and stomack, and yieldeth nourishment laudable enough, yet may I not commend it to such as are affected with melancholy.

Col. Kenney Herbert, *The Cookery of the Hare*, 1896 (quoting Dr Tobias Venner, 1660)

Mountain Hare or Brown Hare?

After she has put on her white winter coat, the Scotch mountain hare *for flavour* against the field, and for the very reasons that have been recorded in favour of the wild-bred, wild-fed pheasant. She feeds on wild aromatic plants, lives in quite a wild state, is seldom disturbed, and really acquires something of the taste of grouse. The species is small, no doubt, and carries less flesh than the English hare or that of the Lowlands, but what there is of it is excellent. Yet . . . very few will allow this. Scrupulously judged . . . the best English hares for the table are those which come from the Wiltshire or Surrey Downs, the Cotswold Hills, the Welsh mountains, the moors of Devon and Yorkshire, etc., for in such regions they feed on wild stuff, thus surpassing those from agricultural districts that are nourished upon wheat and other crops, even on garden produce.

Preparation: Paunching

Under this heading there are one or two points which ought to be mentioned. In the first place, a hare should not be paunched until it is required for the table, *à propos* of which operation no advice can be worse than that given in many cookery books as to washing—even soaking—a hare. The process of cleaning should be conducted without the use of water, all blood should be saved with the liver, heart and kidneys, and when this has been done careful wiping with a clean, dry cloth is all that is necessary. Flavour is lost by washing, while soaking draws out the blood— the very thing that you particularly want to keep in the flesh— and extracts nutritive value also. The question of marinading should now be decided. This is held by some to be advisable, and by others to be a mistake. My experience leads me to recommend the step in all cases in which the animal may come of an inferior breed . . . and also when for any reason premature paunching cannot be avoided.

Col. Kenney Herbert, *The Cookery of the Hare*, 1896

Preparation: Butchery

A full-grown hare is rather a big dish for a small family, so it is wise policy to make two dishes of it by cutting the "râble"—that is to say, the saddle and hindquarters—away from the front portion just back of the shoulder blades. The râble will make an excellent roast, the remainder a salmis, or ragout. It is also as well to note that a freshly killed hare or a patriarch is materially improved by a sound beating with a rolling pin. The treatment should be energetic, but should just stop short of breaking the bones.

Marinade

. . . All the really best cooks marinade both hares and rabbits whenever they consider that the game falls short of being perfect in condition and ideal in age, the only difference in their practice being the length of time game is left under treatment.

A marinade is essentially a steeping mixture which performs a double purpose. It makes the meat or fish more tender and it also communicates to the tissues a delicate flavour or bouquet which could not be communicated to it by any process of cookery. It is, so to speak, an irrigation of the raw tissues of the meat by accessory fats and extracted vinegary essences of balsamic herbs, onions, and savoury vegetables.

The pungency of the marinade and the length of time the meat is steeped are regulated according to the needs of the case, and the subsequent marinades may be taken as representing successive degrees of pungency. Sometimes, where there is a good deal of game and a large household, it is worth while keeping a good deep bath of marinade going, but as the mixture is expensive it should be kept when temporarily done with. To do this, quadruple the quantities of the following, and after use boil them up for five minutes to resterilise them and pour them off into fruit-preserving bottles or large narrow-necked bottles. Add to each bottle an air seal of a good spoonful of salad oil, and keep the bottles upright in a cool place. They need reboiling from time to time and always after use.

Marinade No 1

6 dessertspoonfuls of salad oil (real olive)

2 dessertspoonfuls of white wine vinegar or red wine vinegar. If malt vinegar is used, two teaspoonfuls to a dessertspoonful of water should be used.

6 bay leaves

2 sprigs of chopped parsley

2 medium onions cut in rings

No pepper

Rub the meat down with salt and lay it in a deep china dish. Sprinkle the ingredients round and over it, and pour the oil and vinegar over the whole. The meat should be turned and basted with the liquid every hour or so. This marinade is excellent for marsh rabbits or any meat requiring a slight spicing to bring out its rather faint natural flavour. Also good for coarse fish.

Marinade No 2

A glass of white wine or half a glass of white wine vinegar and as much water

A teaspoonful of pepper ground from the pepper mill or six whole peppers

A liqueur glass of brandy
6 bay-leaves
4 sprigs of thyme
4 cloves

2 sprigs of parsley chopped fine
An onion or shallot cut in rings
A fraction of clove of garlic

Proceed as for recipe No 1. If time is short, the strength of the marinade can be much enhanced and its action hastened by bruising all the above ingredients in a stoneware mortar before putting them to the wine. This is a moderate strength and excellent for leverets, etc. Six hours is enough time for a leveret, but a hare is best left in overnight.

MARINADE No 3

Cut up finely in slices:
2 carrots
2 onions
4 bay-leaves

4 parsley sprigs
6 quartered shallots

Bruise these to a warm colour in two dessertspoonfuls of butter, then add a glass of white wine, vinegar, pepper and salt, and a tumbler of water. Boil up, simmer for half an hour, and strain before use.

ROAST

Skin, draw, and truss a hare, marinade it for a day before cooking in Marinades 2 or 3, according to taste. Roast for an hour and a half to two hours according to size, basting frequently, first with dripping and finishing with butter. To the juice in the pan add some good stock and a tablespoonful of red currant jelly, and make it into a good stiff sauce, which should be poured over the hare before serving. The liver and heart if used should be fried, minced, or rubbed through a sieve and added to this. Serve with forcemeat balls.

H. B. C. Pollard, *The Sportsman's Cookery Book*, 1926

A BREAD SAUCE FOR ROAST HARE

Steep the crumb of a penny loaf in port-wine, put it in a saucepan with some butter, beat it well while warming till quite smooth; add pepper, salt, and currant jelly, with three large spoonsful of cream, or, instead of the cream, substitute the same quantity of vinegar. Serve very hot.

——— Liver Sauce for Roast Hare or Rabbit ———

The liver should be well stewed in brown stock if for hare or white if for rabbit; when quite done pound it with a few herbs, a clove of shallot, and afterwards add to the gravy in which it has stewed a little vinegar or lemon-juice, a glass of white wine if for rabbit, if for hare a glass of port-wine, with, if approved, half a glass of currant jelly. Simmer the whole, and flavour with salt and pepper.

——— Another Liver Sauce for a Hare ———

Braise the liver of a hare raw with a spoon, melt a little butter, with some milk and flour, and put the liver into it hot; add a little salt and good cream, with some of the gravy from the hare. Simmer it altogether over the fire, stirring it all the time.

J. H. Walsh, F.R.C.S., *The British Cookery Book*, 1864

——— Sauce for Roast Hare ———

Among genuine English sauces few are better than a good liver sauce but for this you must sacrifice a most valuable element in the stuffing . . . Good brown sauce . . . may be simply an honest *Espagnole* made on a proper meat-broth basis, but such a sauce will always be vastly improved for service with game when flavoured with a *fumet*, or essence of game.

In well-managed country houses, where game is plentiful throughout the season, there should be no lack of opportunity for the concoction of this valuable flavouring medium, for birds much knocked about, or a hare that has been shot in an ungentlemanly way, will always provide the needful material. The extraction is simple enough: Cut up the game in small pieces, bones and all, and give them a preliminary fry in butter with a good allowance of minced onion and carrot till beginning to brown, then add a claret glassful of chablis (if the quantity of game stuff be about a pound) and a *bouquet garni*. Continue to cook gently till the moistening is all but exhausted, and then add two gills of good broth; simmer for an hour, and strain. This extract will be found most useful in all entrées of hare, as well as in sauces. In salmis of gamebirds, too, it is . . . a decidedly commendable ingredient.

SOME ACCOMPANIMENTS FOR HARE

Cold cooked sea kale seasoned with pepper and salt, sprinkled with tarragon vinegar, and baptized with pure cream, 'onion atoms' or not according to taste . . . marries well with roast game; while an orange salad goes as nicely with a hare as with a wild duck. Peel and divide the orange into its natural quarterings; with the point of a knife make a small incision on the inside of each to facilitate the squeezing out of the pips; lay the pieces in a salad bowl, season with salt and pepper, sprinkle with tarragon or elder vinegar, liberally anoint with oil, adding onion, or not, as in the foregoing. French beans seem to harmonise more perfectly with brown meat than with white, and are of course the natural *garniture* of venison. With the hare they are equally good, whether hot as a vegetable, or cold in salad made precisely on the lines just sketched for orange salad.

STUFFING FOR ROAST HARE

A few words about stuffing. This precaution is important for two or three reasons. It keeps the interior of the animal moist, it preserves, indeed adds to, its flavour, and it fills out the carcase, causing it to assume a better appearance. The usual English stuffing is well known; all I would say about it is, that a little rosemary with the thyme and marjoram is nice, that some soak the breadcrumb in the wine chosen to appear in the sauce, and that butter is better than suet for the fatty element. I have found the following preparation about the best; it is based upon Dubois—*farce à gratin de foie*—Take the liver, heart, and kidneys of the hare, cut them up, and fry them (*faire revenir*) in an ounce of butter over a low fire with a tablespoonful each of minced Portugal onion and carrot, and a quarter of a pound of minced mushrooms. After five minutes' frying moisten with a sherry glass of chablis or sauterne, and add half an ounce of glaze. Continue to cook slowly, and as soon as the meat is soft let it get cold, and then empty the contents of the sauté-pan into a mortar, pounding and passing the whole through a wire sieve. The purée thus obtained, seasoned with salt and pepper, should be stirred into a bowl with the usual six ounces of breadcrumb, minced or powdered herbs, zest of lemon, two ounces of butter, and two eggs. Before packing the hare with this, line the inside with thin strips of cooked streaky bacon. Truss in the old-fashioned way, lengthwise. The sitting posture so often adopted is most inconvenient for the carver, and when one thigh is detached the hare rolls over upon its side—a wreck.

Roast Saddle

The *râble*, as many of course know, might almost be called the saddle. To obtain it the hare must be cut in two just behind the shoulders, and both legs and thighs removed. Sometimes the thighs are permitted to remain. For eight people two *râbles* would be necessary.

Remembering that the pieces not used can be turned to excellent account, the cutting of a *râble* is economical rather than otherwise, the shoulders nicely grilled make, for instance, a remarkably pleasant breakfast dish. I recommend that a *râble* should be marinaded, and contrary to the French custom, that it should be stuffed . . . barded and wrapped in buttered paper, and that it should be roasted with all the care that the cook would give to a woodcock. The flesh, to be sure, should not be as slightly done as of that beautiful bird, but it should be juicy, with a pink colour near the bone, as in the case of the pheasant. Twenty-five to thirty minutes will suffice for the operation. French cooks baste to begin with drawn butter, and finish with fresh butter; the English practice is to begin with milk or broth and finish with fresh butter.

It need not be said that the barding must be removed during the last eight minutes, so that the *râble* may be dredged over with flour and salt, and be browned nicely, the butter basting being liberally conducted.

CIVET DE LIÈVRE

It is often said that the French *civet de lièvre* and the English jugged hare are virtually the same thing, the only difference being that one is done in a stewpan, and the other in a covered jar or any closely sealed vessel.

But . . . there is really no great resemblance between them. A civet de lièvre . . . is a most delicate ragout requiring no little skill and judgement, while jugged hare may be called a self-cooked stew, which any beginner with a good recipe to follow can manage. In the former the juices of the meat are preserved by preliminary frying, in the latter all the value of the preparation is in the sauce, the meat being as a rule 'done to rags'.

Dubois' civet . . . may be given concisely as follows: Having cut up the hare into neat pieces, season them highly, and marinade them with a few spoonfuls of cognac and a sprinkling of sweet herbs for six or eight hours. Then drain, dry and fry them over a fast fire in melted bacon fat till thoroughly *saisis*. Dust over now with flour, turn the meat about for a few minutes longer, and then moisten with enough warm broth and red wine to cover, two-thirds of the former to one-third of the latter. The wine should have been boiled beforehand in a non-tinned vessel or the colour will be affected. Now bring the contents of the stewpan to the boil, and after ten minutes at that temperature draw the vessel back, set it over moderate heat, adding herbs, sliced onions (half a pound) and mushroom trimmings. Simmer now till the meat is half done, when the vessel should be removed, and the *cuisson* strained off. This having been put into a separate stewpan, should now be turned into a sauce by the addition of strong gravy or glaze with some more wine, followed by a reduction, all fat being skimmed off.

Meanwhile the pieces of meat should be neatly trimmed, and freed from any vegetables that may adhere to them. The sauce being ready, put the meat into it with two dozen neatly trimmed mushrooms, simmer till done, and finish with a liaison of the blood of the hare. Dish the civet on a flat dish, surrounded by the mushrooms, and as many small onions separately cooked and glazed. Pour the sauce over the meat, and serve. Observe that there is no red currant jelly in this; that the wine is claret not port; and that spice . . . does not appear at all.

Col. Kenney Herbert, *The Cookery of the Hare*, 1896

JUGGED

This is the sovereign way of cooking hare, but the best results are obtained by dedicating a hare to it immediately on its arrival in the larder. If you decide to jug your hare, it is important to conserve as much of the animal's blood as possible. To this end, then, it should be hung by its hind-legs and a receptacle placed under the head to catch any blood. In order to prevent it coagulating a little vinegar and water should be placed in this dish.

Skin and draw the hare, being careful to clear out the gall bladder and retaining the liver and heart cut in pieces. It can well be marinaded for two days if it is at all old or strong. In any case, it should marinade in Marinade No 2 for at least six hours. Dry carefully and fry lightly in butter, then dust with flour, and let them brown nicely.

Cut a quarter of a pound of bacon in dice and braise together with half a dozen small and tender onions cut in rings and the chopped liver and heart.

Now put the hare joints in a deep crock or casserole and add half a pint of good stock, any gravy from the original frying, and half a glass of white wine. When this boils add the braise of bacon and onions, liver, etc. Let it all simmer for an hour, then add the blood and a dessert-spoonful of red currant jelly, two bay leaves, two cloves and a squeeze of lemon juice. Serve with red currant jelly.

H. B. C. Pollard, *The Sportsman's Cookery Book*, 1926

-------------------------- CÔTELETTES À LA MAITLAND --------------------------

M. Gogué . . . claims to have invented the dish when filling the position of chef to Lord Maitland, "*Ministre de la Marine Anglaise*". The cutlets are neatly shaped out of the back fillets and finished by the introduction of a bone in each of them—either a chicken pinion bone or one of the ribs of the hare. They are then simply breadcrumbed and fried, and served with a plain brown sauce flavoured with a *fumet* extracted from all the debris left of the hare after trimming the cutlets, chablis or sauterne having been used in the making of the essence. M. Gogué does not say that he marinaded, or larded the cutlets. I think that both processes would improve matters, the larding to be drawn *through*, not in and out, and snipped off close to the meat with scissors.

-------------------------------- BRAISED --------------------------------

By this method a hare of a doubtful age . . . can be rendered tender and nice to eat. The animal should be prepared as for roasting, the stuffing being carefully attended to; it should then be placed in a long braising-pan upon a layer of slices of bacon; sliced vegetables, mushroom peelings, and minced herbs should be laid round it; and two gills of chablis or sauterne poured over it. The back must be protected by buttered paper, the pan must be closed, a few live coals should be laid on the lid, and it should be set over a low fire, so that the cooking may be as slow as possible. Every now and then basting with good meat broth separately prepared should go on, and when the hare is three parts cooked the *cuisson*, or broth, around it should be strained and the fat taken off, after which it should be mixed with two gills of Espagnole Sauce boiled five minutes and returned to the pan containing the hare. A couple of dozen mushrooms should be put in and the slow cooking continue until the hare is ready. Serve with the mushrooms round it and some of the sauce, the rest being presented in a sauce-boat.

Col. Kenney Herbert, *The Cookery of the Hare*, 1896

MOUSSE

Chop and pound one pound of hare meat, free from skin and bone. Add to it three ounces of finely chopped fried bacon and two ounces of ham. Work in the yolks of three eggs and half a gill of cream. Rub through a sieve and mix with sufficient reduced Espagnol sauce to form a light farce (test it before using). Season well and fill into a plain buttered timbale or charlotte mould. Cook for forty-five minutes.

Some chopped truffles or mushrooms can be served as a garnish, if liked.

Georgiana, Countess of Dudley, *A Second Dudley Book of Cookery*, 1914

POTTED HARE (1)

Stew a hare gently for about four to five hours with herbs and vegetables tied up in muslin. When cold pound well in a mortar with a good slice of ham. Add a little tarragon vinegar, put into a dish and pour melted butter over.

Potted Hare (2)

Take one hare and stew it for three hours. Cut up three large onions, thyme, bay-leaf, cloves, peppercorns, or any other seasoning fancied, salt and pepper. Put the hare when cooked into a mortar and well pound, and pass through a wire sieve, add cayenne pepper and more seasoning if not strong enough.

Put in a brown pot, pour melted butter over and keep in a cool place.

Minnie, Lady Hindlip's Cookery Book, 1925

Rabbit

THE outbreak of myxomatosis in the early 1950s resulted in the public almost ceasing to eat rabbit. The disease still lingers, but in recent years there has been a limited revival in the rabbit's popularity, and leading hotels and restaurants have stimulated interest by restoring it to their menus.

Rabbit makes a worthy, cheap and healthy dish, especially as a stew or curry. I commend Pollard's recipe for frying, but would use only very young animals, which are tenderer than chicken and fuller of flavour. The carcase should be so small as to provide a generous helping for one person. Use only three joints, namely the hind legs and the saddle, discarding the forelegs as having insufficient meat to provide more than a mouthful.

Rabbit

. . . I have read somewhere that Cromwell—the other, not damned Noll—had it cast up as a charge against him when he fell that he was "of lowly birth and loved a dish of coneys".

The odd thing about rabbit is that, though it may be low, it's deuced good, and, what is more, it figures very frequently on the lunch menus of such respectable clubs that one would imagine the cold grouse would flop off the side-tables at the very suggestion of such a vulgar dish. Now it is obvious that if it was not a popular dish it would not be retained on the exclusive menu.

Rabbit and Onion Sauce

Joint the rabbit and set it in a saucepan, covering completely with well-salted water to which you add a good squeeze of lemon-juice. Add two whole onions and a bouquet garni of thyme, bay-leaf, and parsley. Boil uncovered until all scum has come to the top. Remove this, and when the liquid is clear cover the pot and let it simmer gently for three-quarters of an hour. Quarter three dozen very small white onions and toss them in butter, taking care that they do not take colour. When the rabbit has simmered for half an hour or so take it out and drain it, and remove the bouquet garni. Strain off the gravy from the rabbit into a basin and put into the empty saucepan a dessertspoonful of butter and an equal quantity of flour. Let the butter melt slowly and work in the flour, taking care that the heat is not enough to make it take colour. Slowly, add the rabbit gravy, stirring continuously so that the sauce is smooth and free from lumps; let it come slowly to the boil and boil quietly for five minutes. Now beat two yolks of eggs in half a teacupful of milk, pour it into the sauce, and stir in with the saucepan off the fire (it must not be allowed to boil). Add the rabbit and onions and a little chopped parsley, stir well, warm up but do not boil, and serve.

Rabbit au Paprika

Exactly as Rabbit and Onion Sauce, except that to the sauce is added a full tablespoonful of paprika pepper. This is not too hot, and gives a pleasant distinctive taste and a far more aesthetic appearance than the plain *blanquette* onion sauce.

Rabbit Stew

To two jointed rabbits take 2 ozs of butter and quarter pound of fat bacon. Fry the bacon in the butter till crisp, then take it out and add three moderate-sized onions cut in rings or a dozen button onions. When coloured remove, get the butter really hot, and drop in the rabbit and brown thoroughly, cooking well through and sprinkling with flour, pepper, and salt. Sauté thus for about twenty-five minutes. Stir in a dessertspoonful of flour to thicken, and add three-quarters pint of stock and a glass of white wine. Season carefully with a bouquet garni of herbs, bring to the boil, and put in the onions; cover the pan or casserole, and simmer very gently for an hour and a quarter. When done draw aside, strain off the sauce, remove the fat, and dish the rabbit on a round of toast in a hot dish with the bacon; pour over the whole the skimmed sauce after boiling up once more. Never boil the rabbit in the sauce. It should be cooked in butter finishing slowly in sauce.

Fried Rabbit

Dry and joint the rabbit (rabbits always need a good wash in salted water to disgorge and blanch. This is not necessary if they are properly marinaded); fry in butter till nearly done, then set aside to cool. When cool, cover in egg and breadcrumb, giving in preference two layers of egg and breadcrumb to each piece. Get fat dripping or oil really hot in a saucepan so that it instantly browns a crumb of bread; set the joints on a frying basket and fry them gold brown. Serve on a napkin with fried parsley and rolls of bacon crisped in the same fat and a plain Tartare Sauce.

H. B. C. Pollard, *The Sportsman's Cookery Book*, 1926

Boiled Rabbit Smothered in Onions

Boiling . . . suits the rabbit, but it should be done very slowly, with suet and slices of lemon in the water. The rabbit has a genuine affinity for the onions, and never tastes to greater advantage than when smothered in them. But for smothering, the rabbits should be young and tender, and the butter must be melted with cream.

A. I. Shand, *Shooting*, 1902

Rabbit Catalane

One rabbit, half a gill of oil, two ounces of butter, four ounces of lean ham, one small onion minced, four ounces of rice, three ripe tomatoes, two pimentos, one small bouquet garni, one gill of white wine, one pint of rich seasoned stock and seasoning.

Cut the rabbit into neat joints; trim and wipe them and fry in hot oil over a quick fire; take up and drain.

Fry the ham and cut into dice; place in the butter in an earthenware casserole. To this add the onion; fry it to a golden colour; then add the rice and fry likewise. Next put in the tomatoes and pimentos, cut into quarters; moisten with the wine and stock and let it cook gently for half an hour. Take out half the rice; range the pieces of rabbit in the remainder of the rice in the casserole; add the bouquet garni and season to taste. Cover with the remainder of the rice; place the lid on top, and cook in a moderately heated oven for about twenty-five minutes. The dish is then ready for table and should be served in the casserole in which it was cooked.

Georgiana, Countess of Dudley, A *Second Dudley Book of Cookery*, 1914

─────────────── WHITE AND BROWN ONION SAUCES ───────────────

For as apple sauce has always gone with goose, bread sauce with white-fleshed birds, sweet sauce and wine sauce with venison, and Barberry sauce with the strong-flavoured Italian wild boar, so onions were from the first associated with the rabbit, and with better reason than some of these other accompaniments. For the flavour of a wild onion is the complement of the modest *gout* of the rabbit, which it brings out by some recondite chemical attraction. The discoverer of the secret deserves well of posterity, though perhaps we are indebted for the sympathetic combination to stress of circumstances; for when most vegetables were scarce with us, onions were common. Here is a good white onion sauce which, freely translated into French, might be called *à la Soubise*.

Peel a dozen of onions and steep them in salt and water to blanch them. Boil in plenty of water and change it once at least; chop them and pass them through a sieve, stir them up with melted butter, or roast the onions and pulp them.

For a brown onion sauce, more *prononcé* in flavour. Slice large Spanish onions: brown them in butter over a slow fire, add brown gravy, pepper and salt, and butter rolled in brown flour. Skim and put in a glass of port or Burgundy with half as much Ketchup; or, according to Meg Dods, whose hints are always invaluable, add a dessert spoonful of walnut pickle or eschalot vinegar with some essence of lemon.

BARBECUE

Mrs Henry Reeve, in her judicious work on Cookery, gives an American recipe for barbecuing:

"Clean and wash the rabbit, which must be plump and young, and having opened it all the way on the under side, lay it flat, with a small plate to keep it down in salted water for half an hour. Wipe dry and broil whole, with the exception of the head, when you have gashed across the backbone in eight or ten places, that the heat may penetrate this, the thickest part. The fire should be hot and clear, the rabbit turned often. When browned and tender, lay upon a very hot dish, pepper and salt and butter profusely, turning the rabbit over and over to soak up the melted butter. Cover and set in the oven for five minutes, and heat in a tin cup two tablespoonfuls of vinegar seasoned with one of made mustard. Anoint the hot rabbit well with this, cover and send to table garnished with crisp parsley."

RABBIT CURRY

Rabbit curry is always capital and, if economy is to be considered, the fragments of former dishes may be utilised. The great thing is to make sure of good stock, and the cook's skill is shown in suiting the seasoning to the palates of those who are to partake. Tastes vary; but it is obvious enough that the savour of the rabbit should not be swamped in too fiery a dressing. The cut meat is fried in butter with sliced Portugal onions over a quick fire. The artist must of course pay attention to the colouring, which ought to be soft Vandyke brown or glowing amber. When the colouring is achieved, add a pint of the stock, let it simmer for a quarter of an hour, throw in the curry powder with a spoonful of flour, and stir them into the sauce. When the curry is ready add another glass of cream, with a strong squeeze of the lemon. A clove of mild garlic will not be out of place, and for Indians who prefer a curry strongly spiced add a few capsicums or a lively chilli.

A. I. Shand, *The Cookery of the Rabbit*, 1898

——————— Rabbit Curry, Scottish ———————

From causes with which we have here no concern, Scotland, within the last thirty years, and especially in the neighbourhood of the preserves of great landed proprietors, is overrun with rabbits: they are found useful to small families far from markets. They are dressed in every way . . . but perhaps there is none better than the modern mode of curry. Choose one or two, as you wish, fat, fresh rabbits. Carve each into at least twelve pieces: brown these in butter, with onions. When browned, if you wish delicate cookery, pour off the butter, and add three quarters of a pint of well-seasoned stock for each rabbit, a large spoonful of curry-powder, and one of flour, and six ounces of streaky bacon cut into half-inch cubes, and also a half-dozen button onions for each rabbit: season with a teaspoonful of mushroom-powder. Simmer this slowly for half an hour at least, stirring it. Add what more seasoning you think required, as cayenne, a little turmeric, or some acid. Pile up the pieces of rabbit, and pour the sauce—which should be thickish, as in all curry dishes—over them: serve plain boiled rice in a separate dish. Fresh cocoa-nut is an excellent ingredient in mild curries. Rasp and stew it the whole time: we do not like green vegetables in curries, though they are sometimes used. Mushrooms are an enrichment, celery is good, and onion indispensable.

Margaret Dods, *The Cook & Housewife's Manual*, 1870 edition

——————— A Made Dish of Coney Livers ———————

Parboil three or four of them, then chop them fine with sweet herbs, the yolks of two hard eggs, season it with cinnamon, ginger, and nutmeg, and pepper: put in a few parboiled currants and a little melted butter, and so make it up into little pasties, fry them in a frying pan, shake on sugar, and serve.

John Murrell, *Two Books of Cookerie & Carving*, 1638

Wild Boar

WILD boar have not roamed Britain for centuries, but animals are now commercially reared that do to some extent run wild, eating beech mast, rushes and other natural food.

The boar meat that is supplied today by a handful of merchants is young and does not need marinading, unlike the wild boar of Germany and Italy. Roast it, and you will enjoy the crackling.

WILD BOAR

Can be cooked when young like any other form of pork. With Louisiana or Mexican peccaries care should be taken to remove the glands near the rump immediately they are killed. The joints should be marinaded for a day at least in the following: Braise together carrots, onions, and herbs of all kinds; add one part of vinegar to two of water and half pint of olive oil. If the joints are to be kept in the marinade for more than a day, double the proportion of vinegar. Half this quantity of English malt vinegar is adequate; the recipe is given for proper wine vinegars.

There are two sauces for eating with wild boar, which should also be accompanied by gooseberry jelly.

Cumberland Sauce. Stew two chopped shallots in water with the rind of a lemon and an orange cut fine. After ten minutes strain, and to the liquor add a dessertspoonful of French mustard, a glass of port wine, a teaspoonful of ground ginger, and two tablespoonfuls of weak vinegar. Add salt and cayenne pepper and boil, stirring in a tablespoonful of cranberry jelly or gooseberry jelly.

Cambridge Sauce. Exactly as above, but use English mustard and red currant jelly.

The two sauces are different in flavour despite this seemingly modest alteration. At a pinch just the jelly and and mustard and a little gravy makes a good extemporised sauce and will make camp-fire cookery into a feast of savour.

H. B. C. Pollard, *The Sportsman's Cookery Book*, 1926

Sub Jove in Northern Italy

The first time I tried juniper berries was one night when we found ourselves in the forest, far from any village, and decided to camp out under the shadow of a few large erratic rocks, piled up into a fantastic kind of watch-tower. Our haversacks were deplorably lean; however, we had a fat young tusker with us, shot only an hour or two before. A brief twilight had been succeeded by darkness, and our small fire served but to light up our watch-tower and a small circle about us; all beyond was blackness; even the sky above, with its countless stars, looked dark. Piggy soon lost its skin; the liver, bruised in a pannikin, was set to simmer on the fire with acid wine and a lump of butter (for rich gravy, bruised liver and vinegar and a touch of aromatics are sovereign); to this we added a little meat and then, finding that something more was required, the crackling juniper-branches, sending forth showers of protesting sparks, brought happy inspiration. Three or four berries were plucked and placed in the stew, and the necessary savour obtained.

Guy Cadogan Rothery, *The Badminton Magazine*, 1897

—— LEG OF BOAR À LA PIRENAICA, FROM THE PYRENEES ——

Ingredients. A leg of boar, 2 or 3 lemons, white wine, brandy, salt, a few sprigs of thyme, 1 or 2 bayleaves, pepper.

For the garnish: The cooked bottoms of a few globe artichokes, cooked ham, a little Espagnole sauce, asparagus tips, butter, salt and pepper.

Method. Put the white wine, a little brandy and the juice of 3 or 4 lemons in a deep dish with the chopped thyme and bayleaf, salt and pepper. Lay the leg of boar in the dish and baste it thoroughly with the marinade. Let it stand for a day or so, turning and basting frequently. Then roast it, allowing 25 minutes to the pound, basting frequently. Like pork, it should be thoroughly cooked. When ready, serve and garnish with the artichoke bottoms, stuffed with finely chopped ham, mixed with a little Espagnole sauce and with asparagus tips, previously boiled and sautéed in a little butter and seasoned with salt and pepper.

Countess Morphy, *Recipes of All Nations*, c. 1930

TO DISTINGUISH YOUNG FROM OLD
Birds

Most tests of age are fallible, one exception being the presence or absence of the passage opening on the upper side of the vent known as the bursa. All young gamebirds have this passage, which becomes reduced or closed when the bird reaches sexual maturity. When birds are bought plucked and dressed the test becomes inapplicable because the rear end has been severed to extract the insides.

A simple test, applicable to grouse and partridges but not to pheasants, is to compare the shape of the two outer primary wing feathers with that of the rest. If all have rounded tips, it is an old bird.

The feather test, as well as the other tests described in the quotations which follow, may only be useful early in the season; as time goes on, differences disappear.

Hares and Rabbits

The ears of hares and rabbits tear easily and this is the best test. If in doubt, examine the teeth. In both animals they are sharp and white when young; as they age, the teeth become yellow.

Young and Old

Partridges, when young, have yellowish legs and dark-coloured bills. If held up by the lower bill, it should break.

Pheasants. The spurs of old birds are long and pointed, in young birds short and round.

Woodcocks and Snipes, when old, have the feet thick and hard; when these are soft and tender they are both young and fresh killed. When their bills become moist and their throats muddy, they have been too long killed.

Daily Express, Enquire Within, 1934

To Tell the Age of Game

In *Partridges* the feet are the best indication. Young birds till November have yellow legs, and even later patches of yellow remain between the toes. The first primary wing feather is lancet-pointed in a young bird, and rounded or spoon-topped in an old one. Young French partridges have immature marking, and no rudimentary spur is noticeable on young cocks.

In *Grouse* early in the season the lower mandible is loosely attached to its hinge, and if a young bird is held up by the lower mandible the weight of the body breaks the joint. A better test is the third primary feather of the wing. In a young bird this is shorter than the others and lancet-pointed, and the stem will bleed when pulled out; with an old bird all primaries are fully developed and rounded or spoon-shaped at the tip. Old birds shed and replace their claws, and a new claw or one in process of being shed is a sign of age.

In *Hares*, the ear of a young hare can be readily torn with the fingers, while that of an old hare is tough and leathery.

H. B. C. Pollard, *The Gun Room Guide*, 1930

Grouse

THE showmanship, which for a number of misguided restaurateurs has become an essential ritual in bringing grouse to the table on the twelfth of August, has done this delectable bird a disservice.

Inverted snobbery has led food writers, understandably scornful of chefs who arrive at their kitchens by helicopter or parachute on the Glorious Twelfth, bearing the cargo which has been shot ridiculously early in the morning, to condemn the bird as overrated.

Some people believe that, if plucked warm, young grouse may be served immediately, without the benefit of hanging. I share the opinion of Winston Churchill who, when offered grouse in a restaurant on the twelfth of August, chose steak and kidney pie instead. Even young grouse should be hung for two or three days.

Dead grouse should bear no blame for their final, dramatic journey and, though their dark, strongly flavoured flesh is not to everyone's taste, for many people they are of all game birds the favourite. The strength of their flavour causes them to dominate a meal, so grouse should be given the lead part, and the other courses planned to perform a minor role.

A Love Affair

You come, oh long expected, you are here.
You come, with joy my eager heart beats high;
You, vainly longed for nearly half the year,
So young, so fresh and, oh alas, so dear;
Forgive me if I sigh.

Through Spring, through Summer, oft have I confessed
My love for you, from that I've never swerved;
How shall I serve you? Nay, at my behest,
My menials now shall serve you as 'tis best
You should and shall be served.

I have a cool recess where you shall wait
A little while, and shall not wait in vain;
Soon shall you be with me incorporate;
You shall, I swear it, even as elate
I note that you are twain.

And so my love and joy are plain to see;
My happy paeans echo through the house,
And on next Thursday, Thursday it shall be
Don't order from the butcher, Jane, for me,
Since I shall dine on grouse.

Patrick Chalmers, *The Shooting Man's England*
(from *Pall Mall Gazette*—Anon), c. 1930

A Dream Dinner

. . . let us, for ourselves, imagine a dream dinner. I cannot but think that the principal plat will be game—grouse for me—since I wish to dine, wide-windowed above a summer garden, red damask roses within and without, likewise the last of the sweet peas and, in the high air, the last of the swifts. Clear soup and a sea-trout shall herald the grouse, iced gooseberry fool shall follow it. We (no dream dinner is without a guest—one guest) shall drink a Burgundy—Corton, I imagine, 1915, a noble and gentle wine, warm as the breath of June—and later (to each a soft thimbleful), a Cognac of great dignity and of great age. As for the guest, each man must provide her (*she*, she must surely be?) for himself.

Patrick Chalmers, *The Shooting Man's England*, c. 1930

A Menu for Grouse

Walker arranged his little dinners for eight, which, like Sir Henry Thompson with his famous octaves, he considered the perfect number, on the happiest conjunction of simplicity and excellence. He specially prided himself on one he gave at Lovegrove's at Blackwall: no soup but turtle: no fish but whitebait: no meat but grouse, with some sweets to follow.

'Snipe and Woodcock' by L. H. De Visme Shaw
and others in A. I. Shand, *The Cookery of the Snipe & the Woodcock*, 1904

A Menu for Grouse

A plainly and perfectly roasted grouse . . . is so good that he can in no other way be improved, though of course he may be varied. A certain wise and gracious hostess . . . once said to me, "I have given you very few things for dinner today; for there is grouse, and I think grouse *is* a dinner." The soup and the fish and one entrée ought to be ample when grouse in sufficient quantity forms the roast. Also grouse forms a better "solid" than anything else that I know to finish a fish dinner with—there is some subtle and peculiar appropriateness in its special earthy and dry savour as a contrast to the fishiness. For accompanying vegetables, nothing can equal French beans, which Nature supplies at the right time exactly, and for drinking to match nothing can approach claret, good, but not too good.

The accompaniments of roast grouse, besides those already mentioned, are not very numerous. The liver of the birds cooked separately, pounded and spread upon the toast on which they are served, with butter, salt and cayenne, is often recommended. Most people are unhappy without gravy; for myself I think if the grouse is properly done, not too much and not too dry, it is better without any . . . Watercress is as good with grouse as with most roasted birds, and salad almost as good as with any; though perhaps the brown-fleshed birds do not so imperatively call for this adjunct as the white.

Hanging

It was the custom of a hospitable friend of mine in Scotland, who was equally good with the rod and gun, to keep a supply of grouse hanging till he could accompany them with salmon caught in a river which was by no means a very early opening one, and I never

found birds taste better. The less regarded members of the grouse
tribe will . . . bear much longer keeping.

George Saintsbury, The Cookery of the Grouse, 1895

Hanging

Grouse and its kindred require longer keeping than any other of
the game birds, and hang from a minimum of three days to over a
fortnight, according to the weather and the larder.

H. B. C. Pollard, The Sportsman's Cookery Book, 1926

Packing to Send Away

I don't think anything answers so well as Scotch fir tops—the
common pine, which you can find anywhere and everywhere in
Scotland. Over and over again I have known birds thus packed
and separated to travel in first-class condition from Sutherland to
St Leonards, and I have heard of no failures.

"Idstone", The "Idstone" Papers, 1872

A Preference for Old Birds

In the whole range of gourmandise, there is nothing superior to
the bitter of the back of a Highland bird; it takes rank above the
trail of a woodcock, or the oyster of the pheasant. If I could afford
it, I should like to dine daily for a week in August on a dozen of
grouse, merely cutting out the backs . . . in fact, I have such a
penchant for the inimitable flavour of the heather, that if the age
could be guaranteed, I would rather have well-hung birds of the
second year than those sold at double price as game of the season.

A. I. Shand, Shooting, 1902

COOKING TIME

Owing to their dryness birds should be barded or larded and carefully
basted. They should not be overdone but, if anything, kept on the
underdone side. Twenty minutes should be about the correct period for
young birds. Very high or large birds need rather more.

ROAST

Pluck, singe, draw, and truss as roasting chickens. Sprinkle inside with spiced pepper, salt, peppercorns, and dried herbs pounded together in a mortar. Insert a 1-inch cube of butter or a spoonful of clear bacon fat. While roasting baste liberally with bacon fat or run butter. The drippings should be absorbed on a square of toast set below the bird either under the turnspit or, if they are oven roast, in the roasting tin. This toast is brought to the table with the bird on it.

Fried breadcrumbs, bread sauce, and a little made gravy are served with the bird, which should be garnished with watercress.

H. B. C. Pollard, *The Sportsman's Cookery Book*, 1926

BRAISED

Clean, truss and season the required number of old birds, and fry till brown in bacon fat. Put them into a casserole with a small quantity of stock, a piece of carrot, onion, and celery, and braise for two hours, adding a small quantity of stock or water if required.

Thicken the sauce with cornflour and pour over them. Dish with vegetables in the centre.

FILLETS

After cooking the grouse exactly as in the recipe for braising, remove the fillets from the breasts. Dish these in a circle overlapping each other. Thicken the sauce with cornflour and let it boil till it has become brown like a chocolate sauce. Pour this over the fillets and serve with any green vegetable in the centre. By adding a leaf of gelatine to the sauce this might be kept for a cold dish, and can be made very attractive by garnishing.

Margaret Fraser, *A Highland Cookery Book*, 1930

CLEAR GROUSE SOUP

. . . I never saw a better receipt for it than that which is given by Mrs Henry Reeve. You take old, but quite fresh birds, which may be either grouse or blackgame, or (I should add), ptarmigan. You add water at the rate of three pints to the brace of birds, and keep it simmering as slowly as possible for hours, adding peppercorns and a little onion and carrot. Some time before serving you take the best pieces of the breast out (the birds of course have been cut up at first), press them and cut them up in little bits to add to the strained soup.

SALMIS

Salmis of grouse . . . is probably the best of its kind, except that made of wild duck; and inasmuch as there must always be remnants of roast birds, it is almost a necessary supplement to simpler cookery, besides being extremely good of itself. But it is necessary to remember several things about a salmis. The first is that though the birds are always cooked first, it is indispensable that the sauce and gravy, or whatever you choose to call it, should have a thorough flavour of them, which is not to be attained by merely warming the pieces of game in it. This may be given, of course, in various ways, either by stewing the bones, skin, trimmings, and less worthy pieces of the grouse in the stock used, or by adding some purée or "essence of game"; but it must be attained somehow. The next thing to remember is that this gravy or sauce when finished should never be a mere bath or slop. Madame Lebour-Fawssett says it should be "of the consistency of well-made melted butter" and I agree with her. Lastly, remember that there must always be wine in a salmis; and that it is of great importance what wine it is. A sound red Bordeaux with flavour and some body for brown meats, and a good (not an acid or wiry) Chablis or Pouilly for white, are probably the best things for the purpose. And I must again praise the French lady above cited for recommending equal parts of stock and wine as the main body of salmis sauce. The mixture is added to a foundation of well-warmed and browned butter and flour, plenty of seasoning, including herbs, some shallot rather than onion, and at the last a little lemon juice, remembering the warnings above given. Nothing more but patience, careful watching, and still greater care when the game has been put in the mixture never to let it boil, is required to make a good salmis. But all this is required, and without it the thing cannot be a success.

George Saintsbury, *The Cookery of the Grouse*, 1895

GROUSE À LA PARISIENNE

Take one or more roast grouse and cut them into neat joints, removing any untidy pieces of skin; put the joints into the sauce prepared as below and bring to the boil, then keep it hot in the bain-marie for about fifteen minutes, when the grouse should be taken up and arranged on an entrée dish in a pile; form a pretty border of potato purée that has been forced out of a bag with a large rose pipe, garnish here and there with croûtons of fried bread prepared as below, and serve for an entrée for dinner or luncheon.

Sauce for Grouse à la Parisienne. Cut up into small dice shapes two onions, one carrot, and one turnip, and put them into a stewpan with one ounce of butter, a sprig of thyme, bay leaf, and parsley, and fry for fifteen minutes; then add one ounce of Brown & Polson's cornflour, mixing it with the vegetables, a few drops of Marshall's carmine, four sliced tomatoes, one and a half tablespoonfuls of Bovril, rather better than one pint of water or stock, and half a pint of Espagnol sauce; simmer it for half an hour, occasionally skimming it, then rub it through a tammy or fine hair sieve, put it in a stewpan, and stir till boiling; then add the joints of the bird, re-warm and use as instructed.

Croûtons for Grouse. Stamp out some heart-shaped pieces from some slices of stale bread about a quarter inch thick, fry them in clean, boiling fat till a nice golden colour, then take up and brush over one side with raw white of egg, garnish with finely chopped parsley and grated Parmesan cheese, then use.

Mrs A. B. Marshall's Cookery Book, c. 1880

SPATCHCOCK

A Good Breakfast or Luncheon Dish

Pick, draw and singe the bird; split it down the back and cut through the bone; wipe the inside of the bird with a damp cloth; cut off the feet at the first joints; remove the neck close to the body of the bird, flatten and season with salt and pepper; brush over the inside with sweet oil and sprinkle over with finely chopped shallots and parsley; dredge with a little flour; skewer the bird into a flat shape by means of two steel skewers and place it between a well-greased gridiron. Brush over with oiled butter or sweet oil, and cook before, or over, a clear fire (charcoal or gas in preference to a coal fire). Cook from fifteen to twenty minutes, turning the bird occasionally on the gridiron, and baste plentifully from time to time with oiled butter. When done, take the bird from the grill; remove the skewers and dish up with a sharp sauce (Poivrade or Robert), or a well-prepared tomato sauce.

Georgiana, Countess of Dudley, A Second Dudley Book of Cookery, 1914

————— GROUSE OR GAME SOUFFLÉ —————

Take the breasts of two grouse or the equivalent quantity of any other game that has been cooked, and pound them in a mortar with two ounces of best butter and the heart of a small onion. When you have rubbed this through a sieve, add four yolks of eggs, the white of which must be whipped up to a white froth. Season lightly with salt and a little cayenne. Twenty minutes in a quick oven will bake this. To be served as hot as possible.

Minnie, Lady Hindlip's Cookery Book, 1925

————— TO MAKE A GOOSEBERRY FOOL —————

[Author's Note. Although this book does not concern itself with sweet courses, a gooseberry fool is the perfect sequel to roast grouse, which is why I have included this recipe.]

Take two quarts of gooseberries, set them on the fire in about a quart of water; when they begin to simmer, turn yellow, and begin to plump, throw them into a cullender to drain the water out, then with the back of a spoon carefully squeeze the pulp, throw the sieve into a dish, make them pretty sweet, and let them stand till they are cold: in the meantime take two quarts of new milk, and the yolks of four eggs beat up with a little grated nutmeg; stir it softly over a slow fire; when it begins to simmer take it off, and by degrees stir it into the gooseberries; let it stand till it is cold, and serve it up: if you make it with cream, you need not put any eggs in; and if it is not thick enough, it is only boiling more gooseberries: but that you must do as you think proper.

Hannah Glasse, The Art of Cookery Made Plain & Easy, 1796

Capercaillie, Blackgame and Ptarmigan

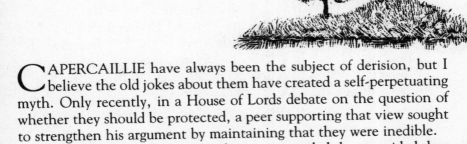

CAPERCAILLIE have always been the subject of derision, but I believe the old jokes about them have created a self-perpetuating myth. Only recently, in a House of Lords debate on the question of whether they should be protected, a peer supporting that view sought to strengthen his argument by maintaining that they were inedible.

An old bird is certainly not to be recommended, but provided they have not sustained themselves too much on pine needles the young are perfectly pleasant, with the unmistakable taste of the grouse family. I once bought a cock caper in Leadenhall Market for a pound and my family praised it. I do not think our palates were too uncritical.

While red grouse rank at the top of the gastronomic league and capercaillie at the bottom, blackgame and ptarmigan occupy a respectable place in the middle. Blackgame, or black grouse—the female a greyhen, the male a blackcock—make their home on the fringe of the moor, among scrub woodland, birch and pine as well as in the heather. If their habitat happens to be preponderantly pine, then they are inclined to be resinous. The reflection of feeding habits on taste is well exemplified on our own ground, where blackgame seem to spend most of their time on the open moor and have excellent flavour. They are, however, dry birds and should be well hung.

Ptarmigan, uniquely, cannot live below two thousand feet, so in Britain they are only found on the Scottish peaks. The shoots of heath plants, berries, seeds, some insects in summer, lichens and mosses, form their diet. Their inferior reputation to the red grouse is based on subjective opinion. The flesh has a bitter taste akin to the back of red grouse, and that is much relished by cognoscenti. Both blackgame and ptarmigan may be cooked in the manner of red grouse.

Not to be Despised

The side-lines of the grouse-moor, the blackcock, ptarmigan, and capercailzie, can be made palatable by Art, especially if they have youth on their side.

Only for Soup

To the capercailzie the great pine woods of Scotland are both home and the necessity of life, since that bird's staple diet is pine-needles and the buds and shoots of trees. Consequently an old capercailzie can, when shot, only serve as the highly seasoned game-soup or "cock-brue". Cooked to any other recipe he, or she, tastes very much as a cedarwood pencil tastes to the author who chews it during the agonies of composition.

Patrick Chalmers, *The Shooting Man's England, c.* 1930

────────────────── ROAST ──────────────────

Capercaillie may be roasted in the same manner as directed for grouse. Serve gravy, bread sauce and brown breadcrumbs with it, and garnish with watercress.

Here is my favourite method: Prepare the bird for roasting and stuff with a bunch of parsley and a bunch of chervil. Cover well with slices of very fat home-cured ham, sprinkle with salt and pepper, and roast in a sharp oven with the giblets around it. When the bird is sufficiently cooked, take it up, remove the herbs, drain the fat from the roasting pan, and add quarter pint stock to make a gravy. Reduce the gravy to half by rapid boiling, pour over the bird, and serve with croquette potatoes and bread sauce.

Henry Smith, *The Master Book of Poultry & Game, c.* 1950

────────── ROAST CAPERCAILLIE (GERMAN) ──────────

Rub the bird with salt and pepper, and lard it closely with thin strips of larding fat. Put in an earthenware receptacle, cover with white wine and vinegar, and season with salt. Stand in a cool place for 8 days.

Roast the bird, basting with butter, adding a little chopped bacon, 1 sliced onion, chopped lemon peel and a few juniper berries. Then add a little of the marinade. When tender, put on a dish and strain the sauce over the bird.

Countess Morphy, *Recipes of All Nations*, c. 1930

ROAST CAPERCAILLIE

. . . An old cock caper is best dealt with in the manner recommended in "Halcyon Days in the Urals":

Draw and clean it and rub the inside thoroughly all over with salt, pepper and mustard; stuff it with onions, sew it up and bung it in the ground for twenty-four hours. Then wash it well and let it soak in milk for twelve hours and for ten in vinegar. After that skin it, lard it well and roast over a slow fire for half an hour. Then steam it for three hours, butter it well all over and give it to the dog, if he will eat it, for nobody else could.

André L. Simon, *Food*, 1949

ROAST BLACKGAME

Blackgame needs to be well hung.

Pick and draw the birds, but do not wash the insides; wipe them with a damp cloth. Truss in the same manner as for a chicken. Place the birds in a roasting pan and cover each with a slice of fat, unsmoked bacon. Baste with bacon fat whilst cooking. According to the age and size of the bird, it will take 45 to 50 minutes.

It is usual to sprinkle a slice of toast with lemon juice and roast the bird on this, which should be served with it, together with rich brown gravy made from the giblets and some bread sauce.

BLACKGAME À LA PAYSANNE

Braise the birds gently in equal quantities of butter and stock. Turn them frequently. When the birds are done, which will be in about one and a quarter hours, take them up, drain the fat from the pan, and add to the gravy a glass of white wine, the juice of half lemon, and a little pepper and salt; boil these together and then pour it over the birds.

Henry Smith, *The Master Book of Poultry & Game*, c. 1950

──────────── BITKI OF CAPERCAILLIE (RUSSIAN) ────────────

Capercaillie is very popular in Russia. The bird is either boiled or roasted, and served with sour cream, or treated as in the following recipe:

Ingredients. One capercaillie, butter, sour cream, 1 tablespoon of grated Gruyere cheese, salt and peppercorns.

Method. Remove all the meat from the birds, carve in neat pieces and slices, season with salt and pepper, sprinkle with flour and brown in hot butter. When done, place on a hot dish and pour the following sauce over them: Put the bones in a saucepan with 1 pint of water, season with salt and peppercorns, bring to the boil and simmer till reduced by half. Strain and put in another saucepan, adding a few tablespoons of sour cream and the grated Gruyere cheese. Stir and simmer for a few minutes.

────── PTARMIGAN WITH SOUR CREAM (NORWEGIAN) ──────

Ptarmigan are common in Norway, and the following is a popular way of cooking them.

Brown two or three birds well in butter, and gradually add three quarters of a pint of sour cream. Simmer for two and a half to three hours. Remove the birds from the sauce, let this reduce a little, and pour it over the birds.

Countess Morphy, *Recipes of All Nations*, c. 1930

Partridge

THE grey partridge is distributed throughout Europe, Russia, and even the Himalayas. Here it is commonly and firmly known as the English partridge, an appellation that reflects the affection in which it is held by country people. The term also distinguishes it from the French partridge, or redleg, which over much of southern England has displaced the English bird in numbers. The redleg has an inferior reputation as a table bird.

The partridge derives its popularity, at least in part, from qualities which the British identify as their own—courage, intelligence and devotion to the family. I once stopped my car on a country road to let a partridge family cross, and they showed no concern at my presence. The hen had marshalled her brood at the crossing place and the cock escorted the chicks, one by one, to the other side. Then they all ran off into the long grass.

An Old Proverb

If the partridge had but the woodcock's thigh
T'would be the best bird that e'er did fly.

The First of September

Sept 1, 1794, Monday. Herring, and his Nephew, Tuttle of Norwich & Peachman beat very early in the Morning for Partridges all round my House, before anybody else, shot several times, and about Noon came again and did the same, went thro'

my Yard, but never sent me a single Bird. A little before 2, Mr
Corbould, with young Londale and John Girling Junior, Mr
Custances Gamekeeper, called on us and Girling gave us a leash
of Partridges. Dinner today, boiled Calfs Head, Pork and Greens,
and one Partridge rosted, and Pigeon Pye.

   Sept 2, Tuesday. Herring sent me this Evening a brace of
Partridges.

Rev. James Woodforde, Diary of a Country Parson, 1758–1802

The Best of Game Birds—the Partridge

He has been canonised among birds alone with his brother grouse,
and certainly, I think, with better reason. At table, on toast, he
excels. Bread-sauce exists because of him; mushrooms and stewed
celery support his sanctity. He comes in with the oyster and the
haunch—and he is superior to either.

Patrick Chalmers, The Shooting Man's England, c. 1930

Roast Partridge

It cannot be too early or too firmly laid down that in the case of all
game-birds, but especially in those which have the most distinct
character and taste, the simplest cookery is the best. If anybody is
fortunate enough to possess in his larder partridges proper, uncon-
taminated with red-leggism, young, plump, and properly kept, he
will hardly be persuaded to do anything else with them than roast
them in front of the fire, cooking them not enough to make them
dry, but sufficiently to avoid all appearance of being underdone,
for a partridge is not a wild duck. He will then eat them hot, with
whatever accompaniments of bread-sauce, bread-crumbs, fried
potatoes, or the like he pleases; and those which are left to get cold
he will eat exactly as they are for breakfast, with no condiment but
salt and a little cayenne pepper. He will thus have one of the best
things for dinner, and the very best thing for breakfast, that exists.

Pudding and Aux Choux

To the best of my belief there are only two forms of what may be
called the secondary cookery of the partridge which bear distinct
marks of independence and originality. One is the English par-

tridge pudding, and the other is the French Perdrix aux choux. Speaking under correction, I should imagine that the former was as indigenous at least as the bird. Puddings—meat puddings—of all kinds are intensely English; the benighted foreigner does not understand, and indeed shudders at them for the most part, and it is sad to have to confess that Englishmen themselves appear to have lost their relish for them.

George Saintsbury, *The Cookery of the Partridge*, 1894

PARTRIDGE PUDDING

This is made like a pigeon and beefsteak pudding but the beef is cut especially thin and slices of hard-boiled egg are included. I am inclined to think that veal would be far better, particularly if combined with mushrooms in the body of the pudding. A very little old black treacle added to the suet crust mixture will give it the celebrated 'Cheshire Cheese' pudding colour and flavour.

[Author's note. Pollard's pigeon pudding recipe is as follows: Either halved or jointed pigeons and then slices of rump steak and hard-boiled eggs arranged in layers in good stock in a pie-dish covered with a suet lining and crust.]

PERDREAUX AUX CHOUX

The name is important . . . *Perdreaux* not *Perdrix* for the latter infers young birds, although restaurant feeders are frequently deceived in this matter.

Take a brace of partridges and truss them as a boiled not a roast fowl is trussed—that is to say, with the legs trussed in. Inside each put an onion, and over their breasts a slice of fat bacon. Now take a roomy casserole or failing that a stewpan, and place in it two sliced carrots, two large onions sliced in discs, three rashers of bacon chopped into squares, a sprinkling of herbs, pepper and salt.

Next take a cabbage which cooks far longer than you will need, boil it shortly, cut it into quarters, break up one of these sections to make a bed or layer over the other ingredients at the bottom of the casserole, and place on it your birds, pressing the remainder of the cabbage into place around them. Pour in sufficient good stock in which the birds' giblets and scraps have been boiled to cover the birds. Bring it to the boil, then let it simmer for an hour and a half or more. Serve either in the casserole or pour off the gravy into a sauce boat, and serve the birds with the cabbage around them.

The technique of the above recipe can be varied in many small ways: for instance, some prefer to cook the birds and the cabbage without parboiling the latter first; others add one or two slices of salmi sausage or a touch of garlic; while some continental recipes prefer a cabbage which is vinegared and spiced almost to the stage of sauerkraut. These are but variants of the main theme, the exquisite transference of flavours from the partridge to the cabbage, and the enrichment of the partridge by the other flavours.

Old pheasants, pigeons, and other birds may also be cooked in this manner with results almost as satisfactory as those which attend on the utilisation of partridges.

H. B. C. Pollard, *The Sportsman's Cookery Book*, 1926

Partridge: Perdrices Escabechados

But there was one dish in Madrid which I shall always lovingly remember, and I give the recipe. Choose a sultry day; walk the streets of that stifling capital; do a round of the picture-gallery and a couple of churches or so; then dive into a dark wine cellar—the counterpart of the laigh cellar of old Edinburgh—and ask for *perdrices escabechados*. They pass you a plate across the counter, with a *marinade* of cold partridge, dressed with oil and vinegar and shreds of cabbage. It is the dish of all dishes to tempt a doubtful appetite on a burning day, and it gives an exquisite flavour to the *copas* of cool Manzanilla, with their far-away suspicion of the bouquet of apple orchards.

A. I. Shand, *Shooting*, 1902

PARTRIDGES WITH MUSHROOMS

For a brace of young well-kept birds, prepare from half to three quarters of a pint of mushroom buttons. Dissolve over a gentle fire an ounce and a half of butter, throw in the mushrooms with a slight sprinkling of salt and cayenne, simmer them from eight to ten minutes, and turn them with the butter on to a plate; when they are quite cold, put the whole into the bodies of the partridges, sew them up, truss them securely and roast them . . . the usual time, and serve them with brown mushroom sauce, or with gravy and bread sauce only. The birds may be trussed like boiled fowls, floured, and lightly browned in butter, half covered with *rich* brown gravy and stewed slowly for thirty minutes; then turned, and simmered for another half hour with the addition of some mushrooms to the gravy; or they may be covered with small mushrooms stewed apart, when they are sent to table. They can also be served with their sauce only, simply thickened with a small quantity of fresh butter, smoothly mixed with less than a teaspoonful of arrowroot and flavoured with cayenne and a little catsup, wine or store sauce.

Partridges, 2; mushrooms, one half to three quarters pint; butter, one and a half oz; little mace and cayenne: roasted 30 to 40 minutes, or stewed 1 hour.

Obs. Nothing can be finer than the game flavour imbibed by the mushrooms with which the birds are filled, in this receipt.

Eliza Acton, *Modern Cookery for Private Families*, 1845

To Stew Partridges

Truss your partridges as for roasting, stuff the craws [crops], and lard them down each side of the breast; then roll a lump of butter in pepper, salt, and beaten mace, and put it into the bellies, sew up the vents, dredge them well and fry them a light brown; then put them into a stew-pan with a quart of good gravy, a spoonful of Madeira wine, the same of mushroom catchup, a teaspoonful of lemon-pickle, and half the quantity of mushroom powder, one anchovy, half a lemon, a sprig of sweet marjoram; cover the pan close and stew them half an hour, then take them out and thicken the gravy, boil it a little and pour it over the partridges, and lay round them artichoke bottoms boiled and cut in quarters, and the yolks of four hard eggs, if agreeable.

Hannah Glasse, *The Art of Cookery Made Plain & Easy*, 1796

An Easy Way with a Tough Partridge

Stuff the prepared partridge with a sausage. Cover the bottom of a casserole dish, earthenware for choice, with about an inch of veal stock, and add a tablespoonful of whole rice. Season with salt and pepper, and a cup and a half of thick tomato sauce, and one onion. (Onion to be removed later.) Lay the partridge on this "bed", and place around it a few rashers of bacon, and, if available, a few mushrooms, and about three ounces of butter dotted all over the bird in small lumps. Cover the bird with buttered paper, then put the lid on the casserole and cook it in an oven for four hours, cooking very slowly. This makes a delicious dish and the toughest bird will taste really good if done this way.

Margery Brand, *Fifty Ways of Cooking Game in India*, 1942

The Little Brown Bird

Take him all in all, the partridge is probably the most popular game bird in these islands. Even the extreme Radical hesitates to attack him, unless legitimately with a gun. He—the partridge, not the Radical—is admirable when alive, and acceptable when dead. Modest and unassuming in demeanour, sober in hue, lacking the pride of carriage of the pheasant and the aggressiveness of the grouse, he nevertheless surpasses the former in edible and sporting value, and runs the latter bird hard as regards the amount of amusement and exercise he affords to the generality of gunners in the British Isles.

The Marquess of Granby, *The Badminton Magazine*, September 1896

Quail

QUAIL have for long featured on British menus, but whereas before the last war they were birds imported from the Mediterranean, notably Egypt, nowadays the supply is from stock hand reared in this country. It is illegal to kill wild quail.

Although to a very minor degree indigenous to this country, the quail is principally a summer visitor from the Mediterranean, never arriving in any numbers. It cannot therefore be regarded as a true English game bird.

Foraging—The Crimean War

I often go out in the very early morning with my dog and gun, and have had fair sport with some nice fat little quail who arrive here during the night, on their flight from Asia Minor northwards . . . I don't know a more delicious breakfast than two or three real fat little quails when, daintily picked, trussed and covered with a vine-leaf, they are kept moving in the frying-pan over the fire, floating about in a gravy of fat from the salt pork.

Sir John Astley, Fifty Years of My Life, 1894

ROAST QUAIL

Draw and truss bird, on the breast a slice of fat bacon, and wrap the whole in vine-leaves held on by a binding of thread. Roast for twenty minutes, serve on toast with the gravy from the roast skimmed of fat and slightly thickened. Alternatively run butter and quarters of lemon may be served.

GRILLED SPLIT QUAIL

Spatchcock the birds and flatten them well; put them in a soup plate to marinade for an hour or two in olive oil, herbs, pepper, salt, and lemon-juice with a bay-leaf or two and finely chopped onion. Take the birds in hand twenty minutes before the time of serving. Let them take colour in butter sprinkled with dried breadcrumbs and seasoning, and grill or boil until firm and cooked. Serve with a good veal or clear stock gravy and, if possible, a sauce Périgord (white sauce truffled).

H. B. C. Pollard, *The Sportsman's Cookery Book*, 1926

QUAIL CUTLETS BORDELAISE

Take six large fat quails. Bone them with the exception of the legs. Cut them in half and coat them with quail and foie gras forcemeat well seasoned. Wrap each half in a thin pig's caul. (Membrane enclosing foetus.) Dip them in butter and breadcrumbs which have been slightly browned. Place them in a hot oven to cook through. Serve them on a fried forcemeat border on a silver grid.

Grape sauce to be served with the quail cutlets. Take some white grapes, skin and stone them and season them with their own juice and a little pepper and salt. Serve them in a sauce-boat with the quail cutlets.

DEVILLED QUAILS

Bone the quails as you would for a galantine of chicken; beat them lightly to flatten them, then sauté them one side of their skin for two minutes, then turn them and sauté them again for one minute. The quails by this means are almost cooked, and in grilling them they finish cooking. To devil them, use melted butter with English mustard and Worcester sauce, and serve them with a *sauce brune* mixed with vinegar, eschalot, Harvey, Worcester. Pass through a muslin and serve separately.

SOUFFLÉ OF QUAILS

Poach some fat quails for one minute. Make a rich brown sauce with essence of quail bones, truffles, and a little onion. Line a silver bowl or deep dish with chicken forcemeat, place in the quails, then pour in the sauce. Cover all over with a soufflé of chicken. Place a band of paper round the soufflé dish. Reserve a little of the essence sauce to serve separately in a sauce-boat.

Georgiana, Countess of Dudley, *The Dudley Book of Cookery & Household Recipes*, 1910

QUAIL WITH LETTUCE

Ingredients. For 4 quail—4 lettuce, 1 slice of gammon, half pint of veal stock, salt and pepper.

Method. Having washed the lettuce, blanch it in salted water for about 5 minutes. Drain well, and put it in a saucepan, which must not be too large, on the gammon rasher. Simmer gently for about 10 minutes, and moisten with a little stock and season with a little salt and pepper. Cover closely, and simmer gently, preferably in the oven, for about 1 hour.

The quail are covered with rashers of bacon fat, put in a saucepan in which they fit closely, and only half covered with stock, and well seasoned with salt and pepper. Bring to the boil and simmer gently for 30 minutes. To serve, put the lettuce on a dish, then the quail, from which the larding bacon has been removed, and moisten with a little strained stock.

Countess Morphy, *Recipes of All Nations*, c. 1930

QUAIL PUDDING

Line a basin with suet crust and cover the bottom with diced steak. Split and clean as many quail as will nicely fill the pudding, and top up with well seasoned mushroom sauce. Add a little more cubed steak to fill up the cavities, and cover with a lid of suet crust.

Steam the pudding gently for 2 hours, and provided you have not chopped the mushrooms too fine in the sauce, you have a pudding fit for a King.

Henry Smith, *The Master Book of Poultry & Game*, c. 1950

Pheasant

THE epicures of ancient Rome prized the pheasant, and Caesar's armies had the good sense to introduce it here. The esteem in which it was then held has not faltered. History records that ecclesiastics, properly aware of the good things of life were, in the Middle Ages, particularly partial to roast pheasant. Thomas à Becket chose it on the day of his martyrdom, and was said by an attendant monk to have "dined more heartily and cheerfully that day than usual". At the enthronement of George Nevell, in the reign of Edward IV, two hundred pheasants were provided for the guests.

In modern times, the rearing of pheasants in large numbers has led to them being eaten more widely than any other game bird. Even if they were scarcer, I believe they would retain their outstanding popularity.

The different breeds of pheasant, leaving aside the ornamental ones, have been so inter-bred that they have become indistinguishable. Only the melanistic mutant, the cock resplendent with his dark, blue-green plumage, the hen dark brown, almost the colour of a grouse, stands out. Of the many birds we kill at Cromlix each year there are always a number of melanistics, and these we select in preference to others for the table. Corresponding with their plumage, their flesh is darker, and they are gamier in flavour than your common pheasant.

Finally, as befits their sex, hens are tenderer and more succulent than cocks. Always choose them in preference.

Letter from the Rev Sydney Smith (1771–1845) to an Un-named Correspondent

Many thanks, my dear Sir, for your kind present of game. If there is a pure and elevated pleasure in this world it is that of roast pheasant and bread sauce; barn-door fowls for dissenters, but for the real churchman, the thirty-nine times articled clerk, the pheasant, the pheasant.

A. I. Shand, *The Cookery of the Pheasant*, 1895

Pheasants

Hanging. In hot weather three or four days may be all that they will stand, but in hard weather and under perfect conditions they will hang ten days or even more.

Choice of Sex. Hen pheasants are markedly superior to the cock birds, and should always be preferred.

H. B. C. Pollard, *The Sportsman's Cookery Book*, 1926

Introducing La Sainte Alliance

But over all these birds, and all others too, the pheasant takes precedence; yet few mortals know how to present it to perfection.

A pheasant eaten within a week of its death is not as grand as a partridge or a chicken, for its whole merit lies in its aroma.

Science has investigated that aroma, experiment has turned theory into practice, and a pheasant cooked at the right moment is a dish worthy of the most exalted gourmands.

The reader will find in the *Miscellanea* a description of the manner of roasting pheasants called *à la Sainte Alliance*. The time has come for this method, hitherto confined to a small circle of friends, to be made known far and wide for the happiness of mankind.

Jean-Anthelme Brillat-Savarin, *The Philosopher in the Kitchen*, 1970 edition

ROAST PHEASANT

Ingredients. 1 pheasant, quarter of a lb of beefsteak, fried breadcrumbs, bacon, brown gravy, bread sauce, watercress, salad-oil, salt and pepper, larding bacon, flour.

Method. Put the beefsteak inside the pheasant; the beefsteak is intended to improve the flavour of the bird and keep it moist, and not to be eaten with it, but it may afterwards be used in the preparation of some cold meat dish. Cover the breast with thin slices of bacon, or lard it with strips of fat bacon, and roast in a moderate oven from 40 to 50 minutes, according to size and age of the bird. Baste frequently with hot fat, and when the cooking is about three-quarters completed remove the bacon, dredge the breast lightly with flour, and baste well to give the bird a nice light brown appearance. Serve on a hot dish garnished with watercress previously well washed, dried and seasoned with salt, pepper and salad-oil, and send the gravy, bread sauce and fried breadcrumbs to table separately.

Mrs Beeton, *All-About Cookery*, c. 1930

—————— ROAST PHEASANT À LA SAINTE ALLIANCE ——————

After the bird has been plucked and larded, it is now ready to be stuffed, and this is done in the following way:

Have ready a brace of woodcock; bone and draw them, laying the liver and entrails on one side and the flesh on the other.

Take the flesh, and mince it with steamed ox-marrow, a little grated bacon, pepper, salt, herbs, and a sufficient quantity of good truffles to produce enough stuffing to fill the interior of the pheasant.

You will be careful to insert the stuffing in such a way that it cannot escape; quite a difficult business sometimes, when the bird is fairly high. There are various methods, however, one of which is to tie a crust of bread over the opening with a piece of thread, so that it serves as a stopper.

Then cut a slice of bread two inches longer at each end than the pheasant laid lengthwise; take the woodcock's liver and entrails, and pound with two large truffles, an anchovy, a little grated bacon, and a piece of good fresh butter.

Spread this paste evenly over the bread, and place it beneath the pheasant prepared as above, so that it is thoroughly soaked with all the juice which exudes from the bird while it is roasting.

When the pheasant is cooked, serve it up gracefully reclining on its bed of toast; surround it with bitter oranges, and have no fear of the result.

This savoury dish is best washed down with good wine from Upper Burgundy.

Jean-Anthelme Brillat-Savarin, *The Philosopher in the Kitchen*, 1970 edition

──────── ## BRAISED PHEASANTS WITH CHESTNUT ────────

The pheasant . . . is a devotee of acorns, beechmast, and, above all, chestnuts; thus in the very nature of things it fitly comes about that though your exotic school of cookery may favour truffles and high sauces, there is nothing in plain cookery which goes so well with braised pheasant as chestnuts. Another peculiarity, too, may be noticed, which is that the little English edible chestnuts, which may be obtained in the same cover as the pheasant, are sweeter, better, and more delicate in flavour than the larger imported nuts from Spain or Italy.

Line a saucepan with bacon and add 2 ounces of butter with which the pheasant's liver has been minced. Put in the pheasant and fry while turning it until it is nicely browned. Take it out and cut it up, then add to the pan small carrots, celery, the hearts of Spanish onions, a bouquet garni of herbs, a shallot, and half a pint of game stock. Braise gently for half an hour. Par-roast your chestnuts, then peel them and add them to the stock to boil for ten minutes before serving.

H. B. C. Pollard, *The Sportsman's Cookery Book*, 1926

──────── ## BOILED ────────

White celery sauce and a plain boiled hen pheasant have a virginal simplicity; but if you make a really good white sauce, with a dash of white wine and a truffle flavour or a kindred cold white glaze, boiled pheasant becomes a real Cinderella.

H. B. C. Pollard, *The Gun Room Guide*, 1930

──────── ## CELERY SAUCE FOR PHEASANT ────────

Two or three heads of celery, sliced thin, put into a saucepan with equal quantities of sugar and salt, a dust of white pepper, and two or three ounces of butter. Stew your celery slowly till it comes pulp, but not brown, add two or three ounces of flour, and a good half-pint of milk, or cream. Let it simmer twenty minutes, and then rub the mixture through a sieve.

Edward Spencer, *Cakes & Ale*, 1897

———————— FAISAN À LA MODE D'ALCANTARA ————————

This recipe comes from the famous Alcantara convent in Portugal.

Empty the pheasant from the front; bone its breast and stuff it with fine ducks' foies gras, mixed with quartered truffles, cooked in port wine.

Marinade the pheasant for three days in port wine, taking care that it be well covered therewith. This done, cook it "en casserole" . . . Reduce the port wine of the marinade; add to it a dozen medium-sized truffles; set the pheasant on these truffles, and heat for a further ten minutes.

N.B. This last part of the recipe may be advantageously replaced by the *à la Souvaroff* treatment—that is to say, having placed the pheasant and the truffles in a terrine, sprinkle them with the reduced port combined with slightly buttered game glaze; then hermetically seal down the lid of the terrine, and complete the cooking in the oven.

A. Escoffier, *A Guide to Modern Cookery*, 1926

———————— EN COCOTTE ————————

Ingredients: 1 or 2 pheasants, 2 oz of butter, half pint of veal stock, 1 gill of white wine, salt and pepper. A few pieces of smoked ham cut in dice.

Method: Put the butter in an earthenware casserole or cocotte and, when hot, add the pheasant, and cook it, turning occasionally, till a golden colour. Season with salt and pepper, add the ham, cover with the veal stock and wine, and simmer very gently for about 2 hours.

Countess Morphy, *Recipes of All Nations*, c. 1930

———————— FAISAN À LA GEORGIENNE ————————

Truss the pheasant as for an entrée, and put it into a saucepan with thirty fresh, halved, and well-peeled walnuts; the juice of two lbs of grapes and of four oranges pressed on a sieve; a wineglassful of Malmsey wine; a glassful of strong green tea; one and one-half oz of butter, and the necessary seasoning.

Poach the pheasant in this preparation for about thirty minutes, and colour it when it is almost cooked.

When about to serve, dish it and surround it with fresh walnuts.

Strain the cooking-liquor through a napkin; add thereto one-third pint of game Espagnole, and reduce to half.

Slightly coat the pheasant and its garnish with the sauce, and serve what remains of the latter separately.

Faisan à la Normande

Colour the pheasant in butter.

Meanwhile quarter, peel, mince, and slightly toss in butter six medium-sized apples.

Garnish the bottom of a terrine with a layer of these apples; set the browned pheasant thereon; surround it with what remains of the apples; sprinkle it with a few tablespoonfuls of fresh cream; cover the terrine and cook in the oven for from twenty to twenty-eight minutes.

Serve the preparation in the terrine.

A. Escoffier, A *Guide to Modern Cooking*, 1926

Flamande

A dish for those who like sauerkraut. Roast the pheasant in the usual way, and when it is done bury it in the sauerkraut and cook for twenty minutes in a slow oven, serving with grilled chipolata sausages round it and its own gravy poured over it. The sauerkraut is prepared thus: Wash and drain well two pounds of it. Rub a deep pan with pork fat, and put in the sauerkraut with a few pieces of thin streaky bacon, half a dozen dried juniper berries coarsely broken, a few slices of garlic-flavoured salami, salt, pepper, and a quarter of a pint of dry white wine. Put on the lid and cook in a slow oven for three hours.

Ambrose Heath, *Good Poultry & Game Dishes*, 1953

Salmis de Faisan

Salmis is perhaps the most delicate and most perfect of the game preparations bequeathed to us by old-fashioned cookery. If it be less highly esteemed nowadays, it is owing to the fact that this recipe has been literally spoiled by the haphazard fashion in which it has been applied right and left to game already cooked, and cooked again for the purpose.

The recipe I give may be applied to all the birds in the two classes referred to.

Roast the pheasant, keeping it moderately underdone. Quickly cut it into eight pieces, thus: two legs, two wings (separated from the pinions), and the breast cut into four lengthwise.

Skin the pieces; trim them neatly and keep them at a temperate heat in a covered vegetable-pan, with a few drops of burnt brandy and a little clear melted meat glaze.

Pound the carcass and the trimmings, and add to them half a bottleful of red wine (almost entirely reduced), three chopped shallots and a few mignonette peppers. Add one-quarter pint of good game Espagnole Sauce; cook for ten minutes; rub through a sieve, pressing well the while, and then strain through a strainer.

Reduce this sauce to about one-third, and despumate it; strain it once more through a close strainer; add a small quantity of butter, and pour it over the pieces of pheasant, to which add a fine, sliced truffle and six grooved mushroom heads.

I advise the discarding of the old method of dishing upon a cushion of bread fried in butter, as also of the triangular croûtons fried in butter and coated with gratin forcemeat, which usually accompanied the salmis.

A speedy preparation and a simple method of dishing, which facilitate the service and allow of the salmis being eaten hot, are the only necessary conditions. Moreover, the goodness of the preparation is such as to be independent of a fantastic method of dishing.

A. Escoffier, *A Guide to Modern Cookery*, 1926

CHAUD-FROID

Braise or roast a brace of pheasants and let get cold. Cut them up into boneless pieces and lay them out flat on a large dish.

From the bones, skin and giblets make 1 pint of rich brown sauce, adding 1 oz red-currant jelly and quarter oz powdered gelatine, stirring well till both are dissolved. Mask the fillets of pheasant twice with this sauce, and decorate with diamond or fancy cut shapes of truffle. When quite set, brush over with aspic jelly to glaze them. Cut out each fillet with a hot pointed knife, arranging them on a bed of crisp lettuce leaves, with a border of watercress and slices of hard-boiled egg.

Henry Smith, *The Master Book of Poultry & Game*, c. 1950

Accompaniments

One eats probably more roast pheasants than any other game, and one gets extremely tired of them. Most cooks forget to put a squeeze of lemon-juice in the pheasant gravy, but pheasant does want a little sharpening. An orange salad, as made for wild duck, goes astonishingly well as a change from braised celery, and quite a lot can be done with variety in trimmings such as sweet peppers and tomatoes. Personally I like corn fritters with roast game. A tin of sweet corn is strained through a gauze till the corn is left fairly dry. This is simply made into fritters, like apple, with a plain flour, not egg batter, and served with the roast.

H. B. C. Pollard, *The Gun Room Guide*, 1930

Wild Duck

FROM the ponds of London parks to the Arctic wastes, throughout all the temperate world and to a lesser extent the Tropics, the mallard, commonly known as the wild duck, is to be found wherever there is marsh or waterway.

This ubiquitous bird, along with the similarly widespread teal, has the merit of being the best to eat of all wildfowl. When England was composed more of swamp than field the huge population of duck, especially in East Anglia, must have provided a good proportion of the meat diet. It was said that the monks of the fens stretched a point, and served the birds on Fridays and Fast days, in the faith that they were as much fish as fowl.

Being of comparable, though smaller, size to domestic duck, the mallard in a poulterer's shop is very recognisable. The tiny teal is less so, but it is equally good. We shot a good bag of teal one evening, and decided to serve them as a treat for a dinner party a few days later. One of the guests looked at the bird on his plate with puzzlement and asked if it was a sparrow.

Other members of the duck family vary much in flavour, depending on the nature of their feeding grounds. The breeds of diving duck are to be avoided in favour of the surface feeding varieties.

Small is Beautiful

Teal, for pleasantnesse and wholesomenesse of meat excelleth all other water-fowle.

Venner, *Vita recta ad vitam longam*, 1628

World Wide

Ducks have helped the adventurous traveller or the hunter through hard shifts on the prairie, the steppes, and the tundras; and in Europe they have given the roving sportsman capital shooting from the lagoons of Provence and the Pontine Marshes to the lakes of Albania and the isles of Greece. Mallard, widgeon and teal swarm on the tanks of Hindustan, and we have heard an old Indian sportsman discourse voluptuously on the charms of the hunter's pot, an oriental variation on Meg Merrilees' Cauldron. It was a favourite dish in the shifting encampments when a party of friends were out after tigers or big game. It was a blending of choice scraps from all the game they bagged with eggs and mushrooms, olives and truffles, working up, in the words of the tramps' landlord in "The Old Curiosity Shop", into one delicious gravy. But my friend said what gave it its most delicious flavour were the breasts of the wild duck and the bosoms of the snipe.

In Europe

It is eminently unsuited to the light wines of the Rhine or Moselle, and I have never come across it at a German dinner table. But when I have bagged my own ducks in the Ardennes and had them cooked in the comfortable little hostelries of the country of St Hubert, I have revelled over them as the dish of the evening, with a cobwebbed flask of burgundy. And at the Hotel of Avranches, overlooking the Bay of St Michael, they had a notable speciality of wild duck, larded with bacon and stuffed with olives.

The Gem

As to the pretty little teal, you are safe with him; he is the gem of the duck tribe and the jewel of the spit.

A. I. Shand, *The Cookery of Ducks & Geese*, 1905

Earthenware Crocks

In the old days wild duck and teal were presented in earthenware crocks covered with butter. The system lacked the certainty of "canned goods", but the contents tasted immeasurably better.

The principle still endures in the shape of the little crocks containing foie gras or "Paté de Merles de Corse", which are imported from France.

SAUCES FOR WILDFOWL

No 1, Fowler's Sauce. The simplest sauce is prepared at the table. The breasts of the birds are scored to let the gravy run out. This is collected and transferred to a small hot sauceboat, or preferably to a little sauce boiler with a spirit lamp beneath it. Add one tablespoonful of port (in emergency Burgundy or even Madeira may be substituted), one tablespoonful of lemon-juice, and six drops of Tabasco or chilli vinegar. Stir it all up and pour over the bird and serve.

This sauce has the merit of simplicity, for it can be prepared at an inn or at fowling quarters where condiments are not usually stocked. A flask of port, a bottle of Tabasco, and a couple of lemons take up little room in one's kit and *faut de mieux* provide an admirable dressing.

No 2, Fowler's Sauce. This recipe was written by Colonel Peter Hawker, and in process of time sauce à la Russe has vanished. Careful experiment by Mrs Haines has restored the Colonel's recipe for modern cookery as follows:

Port Wine	2 glasses
Sauce Diable Escoffier (or, second choice, Harvey's Sauce	1 tablespoonful
Mushroom Ketchup	1 tablespoonful
Lemon-juice	1 tablespoonful
Lemon-peel	1 slice
Shallot (large)	1 slice
Cayenne	a trace only
Mace	1 blade
Cloves	2

The four latter are stewed in a little stock made with the giblets. Butter is melted and flour stirred in to form a *roux*, the stock sauce being then added and boiled to thicken. Cornflour can be used to thicken, but is an indifferent substitute, as wild fowl need additional fat, and butter is always preferable.

No 3, Fowler's Sauce. The third sauce is a variant of the preceding ones.

Salt	1 saltspoonful
Cayenne	half saltspoonful
Lemon-juice	1 dessertspoonful
Pounded Sugar	1 dessertspoonful
Ketchup	1 dessertspoonful
Harvey's Sauce	2 dessertspoonfuls
Port Wine	3 dessertspoonfuls

No 4, Sauce Diana. The fourth sauce is, perhaps, the best of all, for it consists of the modernised Hawker recipe (No 2) with the addition of a full tablespoonful of red currant jelly or more, according to taste, for red currant jelly varies very much in intensity, according to whether it is bought or home made. This sauce should be made to the consistency of cream or demi-glace, and served in a large sauceboat with the ducks. The latter, by the way, should never be served on toasts.

No 5, Sauce Bigarade. The student will have noticed that in the foregoing sauces the main motifs are wine, lemon, and piquante or peppery things, all of which serve excellently to enhance the flavour of the bird and obscure any slight fishiness that may exist. In the same way the flavour of orange harmonises ideally with wild fowl, and though with the foregoing sauces an orange salad is usually served as an accessory, this same motif can be included in the sauce, thus:

Shred the rinds of two oranges very finely, boil for five minutes, drain, and set aside. In 1 oz of butter stir in one dessertspoonful of flour, add a breakfastcup full of stock in which the duck giblets have been simmered and which has been flavoured with herbs, pepper, and salt. Add the juice of two oranges, a teaspoonful of sugar, a tablespoonful of sherry or Madeira, six drops of Tabasco or chilli vinegar, then add the shredded orange-peel, and stir rapidly, bringing the whole to the boil. Serve in a sauceboat.

No 6, Orange Salad Served with Wild Duck. Peel four oranges and skin out and remove the pips from the "pegs". Add a few slices of lemon. To one tablespoon of good olive salad oil add an equal quantity of brandy, half a teaspoonful of sugar, and half a saltspoonful of cayenne. Sprinkle a little fresh chopped parsley or tarragon over the whole. Mix carefully without pulping the fruit, and allow to stand for an hour before use.

Branches of watercress or a little celery chopped finely may be added if desired, but on the whole the salad is best plain.

Perfectly fried chipped "straw" potatoes, braised celery, and really good Burgundy are indicated as the best adjuncts—all suitable autumnal fare.

A SIMPLE SAUCE

Teal in particular and many of the small wildfowl are often excellent with a sauce simply composed of equal quantities of lemon juice and olive oil with a dash of Tabasco or cayenne whipped in.

H. B. C. Pollard, *The Sportsman's Cookery Book*, 1926

ROAST

Keep ducks three days. From twenty-five minutes to half an hour will roast them. Baste well, and dust lightly with flour to make them froth, and look a rich, warm brown. All sorts of wild fowl require to be longer kept than your "tame villatic fowl", because they are drier in the flesh, for the same reasons that a city alderman is more abounding in juices than a backwoodsman or an Indian hunter.

Margaret Dods, *The Cook & Housewife's Manual*, 1870 edition

ROAST

Pluck and singe the birds clean, draw and wipe well with a damp cloth. Rub the inside with salt and an onion split in two. Stuff with sliced apples and truss in the usual manner.

Place the bird in a roasting pan and rub the surface with salad oil and sprinkle with salt and pepper. Roast uncovered at 400 degrees F for the first 10 minutes, then lower the heat to 375 degrees F and cook a further 20 minutes or until tender, surrounded with the giblets.

Remove the bird to a hot dish and serve with gravy made from the drippings in the pan simmered with the giblets. Serve with a tart jelly like red currant, or with orange salad.

Some prefer to stuff the bird with mashed potato highly seasoned with a little minced onion in it, while others prefer the bird sprinkled inside with a little ground ginger.

Henry Smith, *The Master Book of Poultry & Game*, c. 1950

With Port

This is a very good way of serving wild duck, which is rather dull roasted. Put the bird in a flat saucepan and roast it in a very hot oven, not more than fifteen minutes, so that it is only partly cooked. Baste often and season well. When ready, remove the bird and carve fillets out of the breast and best part of the legs. Put in a saucepan a tablespoonful of claret and one of port, very little jus, or stock, and a piece, no bigger than a nut, of butter in which you have worked a little flour, and reduce this sauce at least by half. Meanwhile, put the fillets in another saucepan, pour in a liqueur glassful of brandy and set it alight. Keep them hot. Add to the reduced sauce whatever blood and gravy may be in the dish where you have carved the bird, a tablespoonful of fresh cream, a little lemon juice, reduce again, see that it is well seasoned; add, at the last minute, a few pieces of butter, one by one, stirring well and pour this sauce through a fine strainer (or squeeze it through a muslin) over your fillets in the serving dish.

With Bitter Oranges (Bigarade)

Take some wild ducks, allowing one for two or at the most three people, as only the breast is really good and tender; it should be carved in thin slices.

Put a piece of butter in a shallow saucepan and roast the ducks in it, baste often, allowing about twenty minutes in a fairly quick oven.

Remove the ducks and keep them hot. Put very little flour in the saucepan and make a little roux; add a glass of port wine and one of veal stock; stir well and finish cooking the ducks in that for ten minutes.

Meanwhile, put in a small saucepan a little castor sugar and melt it. When it turns yellow put in a liqueur glassful of curaçao. Add the sauce from the ducks, the skin of one orange (pith carefully removed) cut thick and small, like matches, and a little lemon juice.

Bring to the boil and cook a minute or two.

Skin the birds and pour this sauce all over; serve with it quarters of

Seville orange, carefully peeled with a very sharp knife, made hot in a small saucepan.

The only possible vegetable with this dish is potatoes in some form, soufflés, sautées, Anna or Macaire.

Elvia & Maurice Firuski (eds), *The Best of Boulestin*, 1952

À LA AMERICAINE

Stuff a wild duck with soaked bread, well buttered and well seasoned; braise it and serve it with a brown sauce made with the neck, giblets, wings and liver of the duck. Add some chopped shallots, fried in butter, seasoning and port wine. The duck should not be overcooked.

STUFFED

Braise some wild ducks and stuff with a mixture of minced game and chopped mushrooms. Serve with a game sauce, into which a little red currant jelly has been incorporated.

Georgiana, Countess of Dudley, *A Second Dudley Book of Cookery*, 1914

GRILLED

Young wild duck can be grilled for a change. Split them down the back (the teal, however, should be left whole), rub them with olive oil, sprinkle with salt and pepper, and lay them, skin side down, on the griller. Grill under a moderate heat until they are tender, turning them several times so that they brown evenly. They should take from fifteen to twenty minutes. Serve with maitre d'hotel butter.

EN SALMIS

Roast the wild duck, which must be kept underdone, in a quick oven for about twenty minutes, basting it often and well. Keep it warm while you make a sauce with a walnut of butter kneaded with flour, a tablespoonful of claret and the same of port, and reduce it until you have only a tablespoonful left. Cut the fillets off the duck, pour a teaspoonful of warmed brandy over them and set it alight. Add to the sauce any blood and gravy from the dish in which the duck was roasted and carved, together with a squeeze of lemon and a little cream. Cook for a few minutes to reduce slightly again, and pour this over the fillets.

Ambrose Heath, *Good Poultry & Game Dishes*, 1953

Wild Goose

IN mid-September we hear the first calls of the grey geese, which have migrated south for the winter from their Arctic breeding grounds. Pinkfeet arrive first, followed by greylag.

On the lochs, where we shoot mallard and teal at evening flight, geese often come in to roost. In our valley, between the Firths of Forth and Tay, they have increased hugely in numbers in recent years. To lessen the depredation of farm crops a cull is sensible.

A goose can live well beyond the age of thirty, and such veterans are not to be recommended for eating. A young bird has great merit, but if you do not shoot for your own pot you will need to know a friendly fowler to get one. Wild geese, by law, are not allowed to be sold.

WILD GOOSE

Young geese make an excellent roast, but the older birds require hanging until obvious signs of ripeness are present, and are then if it can be managed better baked in a closed casserole covered with stock.

No 1, Roast Goose—A French Method. In France wild geese are stuffed with a mash of russet pippins and a little sugar, the vent being sewn up. A sauce is made of butter and a glass of mild vinegar or white wine to which a little sugar is added, and the bird is roasted while being basted with the sauce. When done, this sauce together with the gravy and dripping of the bird is warmed up, but not allowed to boil, and a double tablespoonful of gooseberry jelly stirred in.

No 2, Roast Goose. A preferable method so far as most English taste is concerned is to stuff the goose with chopped onion, sausage meat, breadcrumbs, herbs, etc., and roast in the oven, serving with a thick brown gravy sauce and apple sauce apart.

No 3, Roast Goose. A Norfolk recipe stuffs the goose with boiled onions and mashed potatoes and serves it with a red currant and port-wine sauce.

H. B. C. Pollard, *The Sportsman's Cookery Book*, 1926

─────────────── BRAISED GOOSE ───────────────

Truss as if you were going to boil. Envelop in bacon, and flood the stewpan with sauce. Put in the goose with the giblets, and a seasoning of strong herbs, cover with herbs and cambric paper, close the lid of the stewpan and cover again with a cloth, so that the lid may be saturated with the fragrant steam. The same sauces may be recommended for geese as for ducks, though peppers and all other pungent ingredients may be used with a more unsparing hand.

A. I. Shand, *The Cookery of Ducks & Geese*, 1905

Woodcock

THE aroma of a woodcock being cooked leaves no doubt as to its identity. The pungency pervades the house and sharpens appetite. The taste is correspondingly strong, unique in flavour and a proper meal for one.

The old writers on game say little of woodcock, partly because of their relative scarcity and partly because they have always been most populous in the extreme regions of our islands. Until the railways were built, distance ensured that they were unfit to eat by the time they reached the metropolis.

Scattered more widely through the continent of Europe, woodcock were a welcome luxury in the outposts of the Empire. In Queen Victoria's reign a regimental mess in Gibraltar imported them in such profusion from Morocco, that it was said any man might have two or three for breakfast.

The Versifier's Choice

. . . In, say, November when one is, perhaps, eating game twice or thrice a week, I should probably . . . agree with the versifier that

> Though men of lore and letters
> May, faint in praise, condemn;
> A woodcock nothing betters
> Unless tis *two* of them.
> And these, divinely tendered
> Whose juices gently stream,

Are lyrics nobly rendered
Delectable, supreme!

Patrick R. Chalmers, At *The Sign of The Dog & Gun*, 1930

Woodcock & Snipe—The Epicure's Choice

. . . the woodcock, a bird which, at its perfect best, may be preferred by the epicure to any game that ever came from kitchen. And the snipe, on similar toast and in similar "trail" (three snipe equal one 'cock), is his prophet.

Patrick Chalmers, *The Shooting Man's England*, c. 1930

Serve Glowing Hot

. . . I have never appreciated roast woodcock more than in a Highland shooting box, where, from the close vicinity of kitchen to dining room, you always knew exactly what was dressing for dinner. The woodcock should be served glowing hot, and rushed from the spit to the table. How can we have justice done him in a club palace in Pall Mall with scores of dishes being sent up in a scramble, or in a grande maison, where the culinary laboratories are a sabbath day's journey from the banquetting-hall, and where the maitre-trancheur does his listless carving at a sideboard?

An Austrian Menu

I remember . . . simple repasts at the Kaiserin Elisabeth at Ischl, when woodcocks, preluded by venison cutlets, followed trout of your own catching from the Traun. For the hotel-keeper there consented to cook the contents of your own basket, and did not insist on scooping the fish out of his reservoirs.

A. I. Shand, *The Cookery of the Snipe & Woodcock*, 1904

Hanging

The Woodcock can hang at least three to four days and should hang by the neck. Unfortunately his outsides do not always ripen as swiftly as his insides, and an old Irish loyalist once assured me that the only way to be certain of a perfect dish of cock was to put the trail of one that had hung three days into the body of one that had been drawn and hung for a week. The French gourmet relies on hanging his bird by the neck over a clean plate. The first drop on the plate is the signal of its maturity.

Roast

Pick the bird, leaving the head and neck on, but remove the eyes. Truss with legs close to body and bring the head round, screwing the beak through beneath the wing. Do not remove the insides, or trail, other than the crop or gizzard. Roast fifteen to twenty-five minutes, basting with butter. The birds should be roast on rounds of toast, on which they are served. The thigh, back, and brain are all favoured portions. Run butter sauce.

Roast with Oysters

As above (roasted in the traditional manner), but the bird is drawn and the inside stuffed with quartered uncooked oysters mixed with an egg and breadcrumb stuffing, seasoned and with a teaspoonful of lemon-juice, served on toast with demi-glaze sauce.

This recipe needs rather longer roasting than the first, say thirty to thirty-five minutes and repeated basting.

Salmis

Woodcock can also be made into a salmis with the trail incorporated in a butter and gravy sauce and put through a sieve. To this is added half a bottle of champagne and a teaspoonful of good brandy. (This may be sound, but, as a matter of fact, Burgundy is the sovereign wine to drink with woodcock, and champagne sauce seems to indicate a clash of tastes.)

H. B. C. Pollard, *The Sportsman's Cookery Book*, 1926

An Irish Pie

As to the abundance of woodcocks in that country [Ireland], it is recorded of the late Duke of Richmond that many years ago, when Lord Lieutenant of Ireland, he received as a present an immense pie, which when opened was found to contain twenty score of woodcocks.

H. C. Folkard, *The Wild-Fowler*, 1875

─────── SALMIS-LADY HARRIET ST CLAIR'S RECEIPT ───────

Cut in pieces two woodcocks, previously half-roasted, put them into a stew-pan with three quarters of a pint of gravy, an onion with two or three cloves stuck in it, an anchovy, a piece of butter rolled in flour, a little cayenne and salt to taste; simmer for about a quarter of an hour, but do not let it boil; then put in a glass of red wine and a squeeze of lemon. The liver and trails should be braised in the sauce.

The "glass of red wine" is vague . . . Burgundy is better than claret, and Madeira or brown sherry preferable to either.

A. I. Shand, *The Cookery of the Snipe & Woodcock*, 1904

──────────────── DEVILLED ────────────────

The following receipt for the preparation of devils is the best that has yet been disclosed; for in this philosophic and amateur department of cookery profound mystery has hitherto been observed:

Mix equal parts of common salt, pounded cayenne and curry powder, with double the quantity of mushroom or truffle powder. Dissect a brace of woodcocks (if under-roasted so much the better), split the heads, divide and subdivide the legs, wings, back, etc. and powder all the pieces with the seasonings well mixed. Braise the trail and brains with a yolk of a hard-boiled egg, a very little pounded mace, the grate of half a lemon, a half a spoonful of soy. Rub these together till they become smooth, and add a tablespoonful of catsup, a glass of Madeira, and the juice of two Seville oranges. Throw this sauce, along with the birds, into a silver stew dish to be heated by a lamp. Cover it close, and keep gently simmering, occasionally stirring, until the flesh has imbibed the greater quantity of the liquid. When you have reason to suppose it is completely saturated, throw in a small quantity of salad oil, and stirring it all once more well together, serve it round instantly. The only remaining direction is that, as in picking the bones your fingers must necessarily be impregnated with the flavour of the devil, you must be careful in licking them not to swallow them entirely.

Margaret Dods, The Cook & Housewife's Manual, 1870 edition

Snipe

THERE is something particularly good about eating a whole bird on the bone. Of the many game birds whose size lend themselves to this, the snipe is the smallest. And its smallness is in inverse proportion to the strength of its flavour.

For a hearty appetite one snipe is insufficient, two enough. If a feast is planned, roast snipe as a savoury is the ultimate delicacy. I first ate it thus at the annual dinner of a city livery company, the Armourers & Brasiers, in 1953. A soprano sang grace, and the seven harmonious courses matched the setting for an evening of perfection.

Hill Station Luncheons

The writer can recall some colossal luncheons partaken of at dear, naughty Simla, in the long ago, when a hill station in India was, if anything, livelier than at the present day, and furnished plenty of food for both mind and body. Our host was the genial proprietor of a weekly journal, to which most of his guests contributed, after their lights; "sport and the drama" falling to the present writer's share . . . the native Khansama had added several dishes of his own providing and invention . . . his snipe puddings were excellent. What was called picheese (twenty-five years old) brandy, from the atelier of Messrs Justerini & Brooks, was served after the coffee; and those luncheon parties seldom broke up until it was time to dress for dinner. In fact our memories were not often keen as to anything which occurred after the coffee, and many "strange things happened" in consequence; although as they have no particular connection with high-class cookery, they need not be alluded to in this chapter.

Edward Spencer, *Cakes & Ale*, 1897

———————— THREE ROASTING METHODS ————————

No 1, Roast Snipe. Skin out head and neck, remove the eyes, truss as for woodcock, tying feet back to the thighs. Remove gizzard, but leave the remainder of the trail. Thread four snipe on a skewer and roast for a quarter of an hour, basting with butter, and serve over the roasting toast. Dish up with watercress, run butter, and lemon slices.

No 2, Stuffed Roast Snipe. As above, but draw the birds, mince up the trail with oysters and ham, butter and breadcrumbs, and stuff them with this, sewing up the vents. Bard each bird with a rasher of bacon. Serve with red-currant jelly and gravy.

No 3, Roast Snipe. As No 1, but wrap each bird in a slice of thin bacon and a cover of vine-leaves. Serve with bottled cherries in white wine.

———————— SNIPE IN POTATOES ————————

This savage dish is worth trying. Choose big potatoes, cut them in half, dig a hole to accommodate the snipe, less his head and gizzard, put in a little butter, pepper, and salt; put the snipe in; tie the halves firmly together and bake for half an hour or so.

Other small birds stuffed with oysters may also be cooked this way.

———————— DEVILLED SNIPE ————————

Put half a dozen curls of fried bacon in a casserole and put it to keep warm in the oven. Cut the snipe in sections and fry lightly to colour in salad (olive) oil. Separate the meat from the back and carcasses and dip the meat in a devil paste of French mustard, lemon-juice, white wine, and pepper from the pepper-mill. Cook up the carcasses and trail with a little stock, add a glass of brandy, burn off the alcohol, and pass it through a sieve. Place the meat and joints of the snipe in the casserole and pour this thick snipe sauce over it, reheat, and serve.

H. B. C. Pollard, *The Sportsman's Cookery Book*, 1926

SNIPE LUCULLUS

Remove the feathers from the snipe and take out the intestines. Sprinkle a teaspoonful of brandy and sherry, a drop of lemon juice on to the intestines and mash until smooth on a small plate. Put this mixture into the body of the bird into two little pockets which you make with a sharp knife on each side of the breast. If you want to be really extravagant you put a small piece of foie gras into the cavity of the bird, but this is not necessary. Tuck the beak through the legs and body, skewer fashion, and after sprinkling with a little brandy tie a piece of bacon on each breast which helps to keep the mixture in the pockets. Fry lightly in butter. Never use any frying medium other than butter, particularly for snipe. Serve the birds on a cushion of mashed potatoes to which has been added some peeled segments of oranges. Decorate the dish with watercress if possible, if not, slices of orange or lemon all round the mashed potato.

Margery Brand, *Fifty Ways of Cooking Game in India*, 1942

SNIPE PUDDING

A thick slice of beef-skirt, seasoned with pepper and salt, at the bottom of the basin; then three snipes beheaded and befooted, and with gizzards extracted. Leave the liver and heart in, as you value your life. Cover up with paste, and boil (or steam) for two-and-a-half hours. For stockbrokers and bookmakers, mushrooms and truffles are sometimes placed within this pudding; but it is better without—according to the writer's notion.

Note. In most recipes for puddings or pies, rump steak is given. But this is a mistake, as the tendency of that part of the ox is to *harden*, when subjected to the process of boiling or baking. Besides the skirt— the *thick* skirt—there be tit-bits to be cut from around the shoulder.

Edward Spencer, *Cakes & Ale*, 1897

SNIPE PUDDING

Pick, singe and draw eight fat snipe—remove the gizzard and sand bags and reserve the trail. Season the snipe, cutting them in half. Boil six eggs for ten minutes. Take the yolk only and a little chopped parsley and onion—also eight chicken livers, a little fresh mushroom and some thinly cut slices of fillet of beef. Make a nice rich suet crust and line the pudding basin with this, then line with the fillets of beef. Put the snipe in in layers and add the chicken livers, which must be well seasoned with pepper and salt. Add the chopped egg, mushroom and onion mixed so that the basin is full. Put in a ladleful of good gravy or stock and lay the suet crust on top. Cover with a pudding cloth and boil for three hours.

Georgiana, Countess of Dudley, *The Dudley Book of Cookery & Household Recipes*, 1910

GALANTINE

The snipe are boned, stuffed with a game forcemeat with truffles, rolled in oval form, and surrounded with a strip of buttered paper: they are cooked in little liquid (mouillement), left to cook in their stock, then divested of the paper, trimmed and masked with a brown chaud-froid sauce. When the sauce is cold, the galantines are coated with half-set aspic.

CHAUD-FROID

For chaud-froid of snipe, the snipes must be neither too fresh nor too high, fat and having the breasts free from gunshot. They must be roasted or baked, barded and rather underdone. When cold, each is divided into five parts—legs, fillets, and breast piece. The legs, being small and dry, are only used to fill empty spaces, so one must not be sparing in the number of snipe. The parts must be well trimmed and covered with a rich and transparent chaud-froid sauce. The chaud-froid is dished on an aspic border.

A. I. Shand, *The Cookery of the Snipe & Woodcock*, 1904

Golden Plover

A YEAR or two ago, a well known cookery writer began a magazine article, "Plover are now in season!" Some sensible recipes followed. Few readers would have been able to put those recipes into practice for, if all the game dealers in the Kingdom were scoured for golden plover, the only member of the species allowed by law to be killed, I doubt if fifty could be found at any one time. These little birds provide a dish for only one person, so the cookery article would not have given much gratification.

I hope it did not, for the golden plover has become most uncommon and there are moves afoot to place it on the protected list. The commoner green plover, or lapwing, was protected many years ago. I have never eaten the golden bird, though I enjoyed a roast lapwing in 1954 at the Elizabeth Restaurant in Oxford. If the golden's superior reputation is deserved, then it is indeed a delicacy.

ROAST GOLDEN PLOVER

Of the golden plover and the green plover the golden plover is held in the highest esteem, and it should be noted that on the continent the plover is not drawn, but simply has the gizzard and crop removed. Thus prepared they are roasted slowly over fried bread rounds placed to receive the drippings.

In England it is customary to draw the birds and to roast them, serving as sauce half olive oil and half lemon-juice with a dash of cayenne pepper or a drop of Tabasco Sauce added to the lemon-juice.

H. B. C. Pollard, *The Sportsman's Cookery Book*, 1926

───────────── To Dress Plovers ─────────────

To two plovers take two artichoke bottoms boiled, some chestnuts roasted and blanched, some skirrets [parsnips] boiled, cut all very small, mix it with some marrow or beef suet, the yolks of two hard eggs, chop all together, season with pepper, salt, nutmeg, and a little sweet herbs; fill all the bodies of the plovers, lay them in a sauce-pan, put to them a pint of gravy, a glass of white wine, a blade or two of mace, some roasted chestnuts blanched, and artichoke bottoms cut into quarters, two or three yolks of eggs, and a little juice of lemon; cover them close and let them stew very softly an hour. If you find the sauce is not thick enough, take a piece of butter rolled in flour and put into the sauce; shake it round and when it is thick take up your plovers and pour the sauce over them. Garnish with roasted chestnuts.

Hannah Glasse, *The Art of Cookery Made Plain & Easy*, 1796

───────────── Fried Plover ─────────────

Truss 4 plover as for roasting, fry them gently in a little oil or butter for from 10 to 12 minutes, tossing and turning them so that they become brown all over. Take them up, sprinkle well with pepper and salt, dip them in milk and egg batter, and fry them steadily in deep fat for 15 minutes.

Serve with truffle sauce.

Henry Smith, *The Master Book of Poultry & Game*, c. 1950

Pigeon

THERE are few parts of the world where the wood pigeon does not occur, and it is common in Britain. In autumn and winter the native population is swelled by the arrival of large flocks from the Continent.

Pigeons may be shot all the year round, and so it can be the means of variation in diet at any time. It cannot be ranked very highly among dishes from the wild and it does have the handicap of dryness. But in a pie its virtues shine abundantly, where it vies in flavour with far nobler birds.

Pigeon

Young pigeons are not very highly esteemed by English gourmets, and this is more particularly to be regretted, since, when the birds are of excellent quality, they are worthy of the best tables.

A. Escoffier, A *Guide to Modern Cookery*, 1926

Pigeons

The pigeon is essentially a dry bird, and proper basting or sautéing and the enrichment of the accompanying sauce with butter are vital essentials.

H. B. C. Pollard, *The Sportsman's Cookery Book*, 1926

PIGONNEAUX À LA BORDELAISE

Open the squabs down the back; season them; slightly flatten them, and toss them in butter. They may just as well be halved as left whole. Dish, and surround with the garnish given under "Poulet à la Bordelaise".

Poulet Sauté Bordelaise. Sauté the chicken in butter and dish it. Surround it with small quartered artichoke-bottoms stewed in butter, sliced potatoes cooked in butter and roundels of fried onions, arranged in small heaps, with a small tuft of fried parsley between each heap.

Swill the saucepan with a few tablespoonfuls of chicken gravy, and sprinkle the fowl with the latter.

A. Escoffier, *A Guide to Modern Cookery*, 1926

WITH OLIVES

Ingredients. 2 pigeons, 24 stoned French olives, three quarters of a pint of Espagnole sauce, one and a half oz of butter or good dripping, stock.

Method. Divide each pigeon into quarters, and fry them brown in hot fat. Have the sauce ready in a stewpan, put in the pigeons, cover closely, and cook them very gently for about 40 minutes, or until tender. Meanwhile braise or stew the olives in a little good stock. Serve the pigeons on a hot dish, with the sauce strained over, and the olives grouped tastefully at the base.

Time. About 1 hour.

Mrs Beeton, *All-About Cookery*, c. 1930

WITH GREEN PEAS

Older pigeons for this. Tie a piece of fat bacon over each bird's breast, and brown them all over in butter or margarine in a heavy stewpan. When coloured, season them with salt and pepper, add a breakfastcupful of stock or water, and then as many freshly shelled green peas as you want, the more the better, to my mind. Put on the lid and cook gently until the birds are tender (which will take a good time), then serve them with the peas round them. This dish, like beef cooked in the same way, gives the peas an unsuspected and quite ineffable flavour.

Ambrose Heath, *Good Poultry & Game Dishes*, 1953

COMPÔTE

Truss two fat, tender pigeons as for roasting. Place them in a casserole with two ounces of fresh butter. Let them colour over a sharp fire, and add two ounces of streaky bacon cut into small pieces, six or eight small onions, carrots and turnip and small button mushrooms. Fry all together for a few minutes and add a bouquet and some small green peas. Place the cover on the casserole, and let cook gently in the oven for about three-quarters of an hour, or until the contents are tender. Skim off the fat, and add one tablespoonful of brown sauce, and one tablespoonful of tomato sauce. Let it simmer for ten minutes. Remove the bouquet, but serve the pigeons and the vegetables in the casserole.

Georgiana, Countess of Dudley, A Second Dudley Book of Cookery, 1914

PIGEONS EN FRICANDEAU

Split four pigeons each in half and lay them in a casserole on a bed of chopped leeks. Cover each half bird with a small slice of bacon, sprinkle with salt and pepper and three-quarters cover with veal stock. Cover closely, and cook in the oven from 25 to 35 minutes, when they should be done.

Strain off the liquor into a saucepan and reduce by rapid boiling to half its volume. Pour it back over the birds and serve in the casserole in which they were cooked.

FRIED

Dip four young pigeons in clarified butter and dredge with flour.

Dice 4 oz bacon and place in a heavy frying pan with the pigeons, season with salt and pepper and turn and toss them about until they are nicely browned all over which, if the heat has not been too fierce, will be in about 20 to 25 minutes. Now take them up, dip them in batter, and fry them in deep hot fat.

Serve with brown gravy and redcurrant jelly.

En Papillotes

Split four young pigeons down the back and fill them with liver sausage rubbed down with a little butter and finely minced onion. Season well with salt and pepper and dip each bird in olive oil.

Grease four sheets of greaseproof paper, lay a sprig of thyme and parsley on each and lay the bird in the centre. Enfold the birds in the paper, giving the ends a good twist to prevent the escape of steam. Bake the birds in an oven at 425 degrees F from 30 to 40 minutes. Send to table in the paper without any sauce.

Henry Smith, *The Master Book of Poultry & Game*, c. 1950

Pigeonneaux en Crapaudine

Cut the young pigeons horizontally in two, from the apex of the breast to the wings. Open them; flatten them slightly; season them; dip them in melted butter, roll them in breadcrumbs, and grill them gently.

Serve a devilled sauce at the same time.

Pigeonneaux en Compôte

Fry in butter two oz of blanched, salted breast of pork and two oz of raw mushrooms, peeled and quartered. Drain the bacon and the mushrooms, and set the squabs, trussed as for an entrée, to fry in the same butter.

Withdraw them when they are brown; drain them of butter; swill with half a glassful of white wine; reduce the latter and add sufficient brown stock and half-glaze sauce (tomatéd), in equal quantities, to cover the birds. Plunge them into this sauce, with a faggot, and simmer until they are cooked and the sauce is reduced to half.

This done, transfer the squabs to another saucepan; add the pieces of bacon, the mushrooms, and six small onions glazed with butter, for each bird; strain the sauce over the whole through a fine sieve; simmer for ten minutes more, and serve very hot.

A. Escoffier, *A Guide to Modern Cookery*, 1926

To Boil Pigeons with Rice, on the French Fashion

Fit them to boil, and put into their bellies sweet herbs, viz. parsley, tops of young thyme: and put them into a pipkin, with as much mutton broth as will cover them, a piece of whole mace, a little whole pepper: boil all these together until your pigeons be tender. Then take them off the fire, and skim off the fat clean from the broth, with a spoon, for otherwise it will make it to taste rank. Put in a piece of sweet butter: season it with verjuice, nutmeg and a little sugar: thicken it with rice boiled in sweet cream. Garnish your dish with preserved barberries and skirret roots, being boiled with verjuice and butter.

John Murrell, *A New Book of Cookerie*, 1638

Casserole of Pigeon

Joint and fry in butter, then put in a casserole with fried shallots, herbs, a pound of mushrooms, a glass of sherry, half pint of stock, and seasoning. Either prepare a demi-glaze sauce from the gravy or stock or add a thick brown sauce made with butter, flour, and good gravy. Mushroom powder (Fortnum & Mason's) can be used with milk, flour, and butter to produce a good quickly extemporised savoury sauce. Time about thirty-five minutes.

H. B. C. Pollard, *The Sportsman's Cookery Book*, 1926

Salmon

AS cookery writers habitually recommend too short a time for the roasting of game birds, so do they by contrast advocate far too long for the boiling of salmon.

My wife cooks salmon perfectly, and this she does by immersing it in cold water in a fish kettle, bringing it to the boil and allowing it to simmer for four minutes. It is then removed from the stove and, if it is to be served cold, allowed to cool in the kettle for twenty minutes. This timing applies to fish up to seven pounds in weight, which is big enough for most people and certainly an approximate maximum size consistent with delicacy of flavour. For larger weights, there must be some discretion in allowing simmering for a few more minutes. Though salmon is an oily fish, it can lose its moisture, so there is advantage in adding two ounces of clarified butter to the water.

It is important that the kettle should fit the fish. If the kettle is too large for it, wrap the salmon in tin foil. If on the other hand, the salmon is too large, cut it into lengths and wrap each length in foil. In the absence of a fish kettle a large saucepan will then suffice. The pieces can be cunningly joined subsequently, the joints concealed by decoration.

Some people judge hen fish to be better than cocks, and certainly their smaller heads and thicker necks make them more attractive to the eye. Whatever the sex, if the body of the fish has great "depth" or thickness, it will need extra cooking time.

On most occasions a whole salmon will not be needed, and when selecting a portion from the fishmonger ask for the tailpiece. That has the best flavour, perhaps because it has the highest proportion of bone.

A number of anglers, who have experience of different rivers, and people who have eaten salmon in homes or hostelries in different parts of the country, profess to discriminate between the quality of fish from the several waters they are acquainted with. Subtlety of palate they may have, but for us lesser mortals a fresh run salmon from a clean river is excellent no matter what part of the country it comes from.

A word for the salmon farmers must not be omitted. They have performed a great service in bringing down the price of the commodity to a reasonable level. The quality of farmed salmon is good, though the sedentary life it leads sometimes causes lack of muscle growth, and in consequence the flesh is flaky, compared to wild fish.

The Tweed Kettle, c. 1786

It is customary for the gentlemen who live near the Tweed to entertain their neighbours with a *fête champêtre*, which they call giving "a kettle of fish". Tents or marquees are pitched near the flowery banks of the river, on some grassy plain; a fire is kindled, and live salmon thrown into boiling kettles. The fish, thus prepared, is very firm, and accounted a most delicious food. Everything in season is added to furnish a luxurious cold dinner; and wine, music, and dancing on the green, steal one day from the plodding cares or more unsupportable languor of mortals. The simple rustics around are admitted, in due place and order, to this rural banquet, and all nature wears the countenance of joy and gladness. Where the Tweed forms the boundary between England and Scotland, the English gentlemen and ladies cross the river in boats, to attend the annual feast of their Scottish neighbours; and the Scottish ladies and gentlemen, in like manner, pay due respect on similar occasions, to their neighbours in England. How different this humane and happy intercourse from the meeting of the Scots and English in former times, whether accidental, or for the express purpose of settling disputes.

Thomas Thornton, A *Sporting Tour*, 1804

The Versatile Fish-Kettle

No modern shop keeps fish-kettles other than those built to hold turbot or fish of indecent girth. If you live in a salmon country, it is worth while getting a local smith to make a proper long fish-kettle of copper such as one gets in Brittany. Draw an immoderate fish in an oversize on paper and make the kettle 8 inches deep and well tinned inside and you have a culinary vessel that might well be an heirloom.

. . . It will also serve for jam making, the steaming of stuffed vegetable marrows, and a variety of mundane purposes, and, acquired in doubt, beomes a valuable and trusted stand-by. If you are likely to have a few whole fish to cook, then . . . get a decent fish-kettle built rather than martyr a beast of beauty to serve in gobbets because of an ill-equipped kitchen.

General Rule of Cookery

There is one plain and simple rule about salmon which should be remembered by every cook. Salmon has a particular and specific virtue of its own. It is best plain, so do not attempt to better it. A clean-run spring salmon perfectly cooked is perfection in itself, and, incidentally, no bad test of a cook's skill, for it requires judgement to boil a big fish so that it is properly cooked right through to the backbone, and the outside not boiled to the amorphous consistency of house-flannel.

Crimping

The angler who kills a fish should decide as soon as it is safely landed if he is going to eat it without delay. If so, he should be prepared to sacrifice the pleasure of displaying an unbroken silver side to the less aesthetic pleasure of preparing a noble fish perfectly for the table. He should crimp it there and then. This process is simple. Kill the fish, then with the small blade of a pocket knife cut fairly deep incisions from the back to the belly at two-inch intervals along both sides. Be careful to cut out well below the gills. Now hang it up by the tail to drain for ten minutes or so, then let it soak for at least a quarter of an hour in cold water, preferably the river it was caught in. A salmon so crimped requires cooking for only ten minutes or so in fiercely boiling water, as the cuts enable the boiling water to penetrate deeply into the tissues.

Salmon to be sent away should not be crimped.

Sealing and Boiling

Now, taking salmon, there is very, very little to be said about it. Clean carefully, scale carefully, and rinse afterwards with a rub down with a cloth in several changes of cold water. This elementary procedure is often neglected, but you will agree with me that salmon scales loose in the sauce are a nuisance and a reproach to the cook.

A fish complete will stand a full two hours of careful simmering, a section of thin steak will not need more than twenty minutes, but in any case the fish needs to be steamed or boiled. Overboiled salmon is abominally flannelly, while "underdone" is a shortcoming that can be masked. It is therefore wise to err on the merciful side.

To Make a Court Bouillon

A court bouillon is a bath deep enough to accommodate the victim, which is filled with, preferably, equal proportions of water and any kind of white wine, or, if economy is of great import, a half-glass of white wine vinegar (of French, not English origin) may be used instead of the wine. Add to the bath salt, pepper—out of a pepper mill, not the messy arrowroot-adulterated product of the godless grocer—chopped parsley, thyme, bay-leaves, a few cloves, and a small onion cut in slices. Boil this brew up for about half an hour and then put the fish in, but simmer it *very* gently or the skin will break in an unsightly manner. In many cases it will serve to place fish in a dish of already prepared court bouillon and raise it from cold, cooking it so long as is necessary in the concoction.

. . . If your cook cooks fish tough, make her raise them in water from cold. It cannot do any harm and will probably solve the mystery.

The Use of Court Bouillon

The French cook . . . is cynical. If we examine the continental mode, we find that two-thirds of their best cookery is rooted in distrust. They do not expect their fish to be idyllic creatures of the dryad-haunted stream, and they do not cook in what a seasoned microscopist calls tap-water, but in a court bouillon.

Now, court bouillon is really one of the fundamental things. It does not perhaps, apply to the ideal trout caught in perfect condition and perfect water on the best of Farlow's tackle, but it does apply to ninety-nine per cent of the ordinary trout, and can be used with benefit on salmon too. It makes just that wonderful redeeming difference between a really successful plain dish and a passable one.

Hollandaise Sauce

First of all, Sauce Hollandaise is far better and richer [than mayonnaise], easier to make, and more difficult to serve. A cook in the real sense of the word will make no bones about keeping a party waiting for a Hollandaise . . .

Was it not the incomparable Brioche who complained to his master that a perfectly served dinner was beyond hope until the Marquis de Trey was better fitted by his dentist? "In order to compensate for the iniquitous delay caused by the Marquis and his plate I must delay two minutes. It is you, M'sieur Le Duc, who must make the conversation, but it is my sauces which will congeal."

Take two yolks of egg, a pinch of salt, half a teaspoonful of wine vinegar, and about as much butter as egg. Put these into a little pot or jar standing in a saucepan of boiling water, stir with a fork until it blends, and serve at once and very hot. It will spoil if it boils, and it will even do this in a water-jacketed boiler if you are not very alert.

Grilled Salmon Steak or Trout Maître d'Hotel

For grilled salmon steak or trout nothing surpasses Maître d'Hôtel. Put a walnut-sized piece of butter in a pan and let it melt but not boil. Add chopped fennel or chopped parsley, pepper and salt, and a dessertspoonful of lemon juice. Balls of butter made up cold with the same formula may be added to each fish before dishing up.

H. B. C. Pollard, *The Sportsman's Cookery Book*, 1926

---------------- COLD SAVOURY ----------------

Make a foundation of cold purée of salmon—then cut circles of bread
(from one inch to one and half across). Cover each alternately with
grated yellow of egg, white of egg, and caviar and a little grated parsley
over the whole.

Georgiana, Countess of Dudley, *The Dudley Book of Cookery*, 1910

-------- USING UP SALMON FOR A SECOND DRESSING --------

No 1, Kedgeree. For Kedgeree, boil half a pound of rice; dry before the
fire: boil two eggs for ten minutes, peel and mince them. Heat a
saucepan: with a piece of butter put in the salmon, then the rice and
eggs. Season with salt and pepper: mix lightly with a fork, and serve as
hot as possible.

No 2, Soused. Souse the salmon in half a pint of vinegar, with salt,
pepper, cayenne, peppercorns, clove, mace, and a shred or two of
garlic. Boil for ten minutes, then let it cool. Strain the vinegar on it,
leave it in pickle for twelve hours, and serve with fresh fennel.

A. I. Shand, *The Cookery of the Salmon*, 1898

---------------- CROQUETTES ----------------

Mash together remnants of cooked salmon and an equal quantity of
boiled potatoes. Season with salt and pepper, a little grated nutmeg and
add a small amount of onion finely chopped, and melted in butter. Mix
well, pound the mixture and add to it a little fresh cream, the yolk of
one egg and the white well whipped. This would do for eight or ten
croquettes, which you shape like little balls, roll lightly in flour and fry
in hot fat, like any fritter.

---------------- TERRINE ----------------

This dish is served cold and in the terrine. It is advisable to make it for
about eight people or to serve it twice; it will keep quite well for two
days in a cool place.

Take two and a half pounds of salmon, cut the best parts of it in fillets about one inch thick and four inches long, and put these in a dish for two hours with salt, pepper, a bay leaf and two glasses of sherry, turning them occasionally.

Have the flesh of some fish pounded and passed through a wire sieve (say two whitings and a slice of cod for our quantity of salmon); mash also the rest of the salmon; mix together, add salt, pepper, a piece of stale bread dipped in milk, two yolks of eggs, a few very small pieces of butter and, if you like, one truffle finely chopped.

Moisten with some of the sherry in which the salmon has soaked, butter the terrine and fill it—first a layer of minced fish, then a layer of salmon, and so on till it is full, finished by a layer of minced fish.

Cook with the lid on about an hour and a quarter in a moderate oven.

Serve this with a plain green salad and no mayonnaise, as it would drown the delicate taste of the pâté.

Elvia and Maurice Firuski (eds), *The Best of Boulestin*, 1952

Pudding (Swedish)

This is made with salt salmon, prepared by rubbing the fish thoroughly with salt and letting it stand for 24 hours.

The ingredients are: 1 lb of salt salmon, 1½ lbs of boiled potatoes, 3 breakfast cups of milk, 2 tablespoons of breadcrumbs, 1 teaspoon of butter, 3 eggs.

Slice the salmon and the potatoes and put alternate layers in a pie dish, beginning and ending with the potatoes. Whip the eggs and milk together and pour over the pudding with 1 teaspoon of melted butter. Sprinkle with breadcrumbs and bake in a moderate oven for about 30 minutes. Serve with melted butter.

Countess Morphy, *Recipes of All Nations*, c. 1930

Cutlets

No 1. Make a salpicon with the following ingredients: a pound of salmon, half a pound of cooked mushrooms, four ounces of shelled shrimps, two ounces of truffles. The binding sauce should be a very much reduced Béchamel, with six egg-yolks added for every pint and three-quarters. The proportion of sauce to salpicon is just over half a pint to each pound of salpicon. Mix the salpicon with the sauce, pour it out on a dish and spread it. Brush over the surface with butter, and let it get cold.

No 2. Divide the mixture into portions weighing about two ounces or a little over, and shape them into rectangles, ovals, or cutlets, according to the description on the menu. Egg-and-breadcrumb them, using very fine crumbs. Keep them in a cool place, if they have long to wait. When ready to serve them, plunge them into very hot fat, drain them on a cloth, and serve them in a circle with fried parsley in the middle. Hand the appropriate sauce with them.

Ambrose Heath, *Madame Prunier's Fish Cookery Book*, 1938

POTTED

This is an old recipe and makes a delicious filling for sandwiches. Butter the entire interior of an earthenware crock, having a well-fitting lid. Place in it slices of fresh salmon together with a few peppercorns, salt, a pinch of mace and allspice to taste, quantities depending, naturally, on the amount of fish being potted. Add a little good fish stock, about one inch in depth, to prevent burning. Put on a lid, covering with paper and a weight. Cook for an hour or more in a moderate oven, then let it cool in the crock. Remove fish when cold, drain on a sieve, add, if necessary, more salt and pepper, remove skin and all bones and pound flesh in a mortar with a little clarified butter. Press through a fine sieve and put into pots, covering with a thin layer of clarified butter. If desired, the flavour may be greatly enhanced by the addition of a little raw or blanched lobster spawn or a little essence of shrimps.

André L. Simon, *Fish*, 1940

FRENCH TART

Remove the skin from a slice of salmon of moderate thickness and cut it into neat fillets. Free the trimmings from skin and bone, and pound them in a mortar with a few chopped mushrooms and about an ounce of butter. When smooth, incorporate two tablespoonfuls of creamy Bechamel Sauce, and season with salt, pepper and aromatic spice. Line a flan or French tart mould, placed on a baking sheet, with plain short-crust paste; pinch the bottom with a fork and spread over the prepared mixture. Upon this arrange neatly the fillets of salmon; sprinkle over some chopped parsley and seasoning, some lemon juice and oiled butter; cover with a layer of puff paste; ornament the surface with the aid of a knife, and brush over with beaten egg-yolk. Bake in a moderate oven for forty minutes. Remove the cover carefully and take off the fat which has accumulated. Have ready a ragoût of prawns or large shrimps, which place on the top of the salmon fillets. Replace the paste crust cover, dish up, and serve very hot.

Georgiana Countess of Dudley, *A Second Dudley Book of Cookery*, 1914

The Curd in Salmon

I really must tell you about sending as a present an absolutely fresh salmon without explaining the curd, the cloudy jelly which goes liquid and is not seen unless the fish is cooked within twenty-four hours or less of its being caught. As a bachelor in the nineties I was most anxious to send the best possible salmon to a house where I had often received the kindest hospitality. At five o'clock one frosty March morning I caught a perfect spring fish of 15 lb, and by packing him at once caught the six-thirty train to London, and he was delivered before breakfast with a message to have him cooked at once. My friend was a hunting man, but no fisher, and he told me a few days later that the fish arrived bad and had to be thrown away. I said it could not go bad within a week at least, and more especially in frosty weather. But he said that his cook, who was a Frenchman, had cooked it at once and sent for him to look at it, and that on opening the fish it was full of a nasty cloudy mould— the curd that I had taken such pains to get for him. He does not know to this day that he threw away a fish such as money could not buy in London.

A. H. Chaytor, *Letters to a Salmon Fisher's Sons*, 1910

Sea Trout

S EA trout, inelegantly termed salmon trout by fishmongers, is a finer flavoured fish than salmon and the flesh is firmer. They are usually cheaper to buy than salmon.

Most sea trout are between one and a half and four pounds in weight, so are ideal for a family. They may be cooked in the same way as salmon.

Freshly Caught and Cooked

Evan and his attendant now returned slowly along the beach, the latter bearing a large salmon-trout, the produce of the morning's sport, together with the angling rod . . . Evan intimated his commands that the fish should be prepared for breakfast. A spark from the lock of his pistol produced a light, and a few withered fir branches were quickly in flame, and as speedily reduced to hot embers, on which the trout was broiled in large slices. To crown the repast, Evan produced from the pocket of his short jerkin a large scallop shell, and from under the folds of his plaid a ram's horn full of whisky.

Sir Walter Scott, Waverley, 1814

The Camp Fire

Some weary of fish at every meal, but I was always able to relish such fare, giving a preference to the delicate flavoured sea-trout over the richer flesh of salmon. But to appreciate sea-trout thoroughly, they should be eaten in picnic fashion on the bank just after they have been taken out of the water. What meals I recall by Irish loughs and Scotch and Scandinavian rivers! Cook your fish in paper on ashes or a hot stone, toast them on juniper forks, or boil them in a huge pot with plenty of salt, and you will find them delicious.

A. E. Gathorne-Hardy, *My Happy Hunting Grounds*, 1914

The Sea Trout

There is nothing to touch him for real liveliness, for silvery beauty, or for delicacy of flesh. I would rather fish for him, catch him, eat him, than any other fish that swims.

Hilda Murray, *Echoes of Sport*, 1910

SEA TROUT AU VIN DE CHAMPAGNE

Partly separate the fillets from the bone, on the upper side of the trout, and slip a piece of butter the size of a walnut under the fillets. Lay the fish in a dish, the bottom of which should be buttered, add chopped onion and two wineglassfuls of champagne, also a little of the fish liquor and two or three white mushrooms. Let this poach gently. Lay the fish on its dish to serve.

Take the liquid and let it reduce, adding two large spoonfuls of white velouté sauce and a little thick cream. Strain the sauce through muslin or tammy—season it nicely. Serve with quenelles of lobster.

Georgiana, Countess of Dudley, *The Dudley Book of Cookery & Household Recipes*, 1910

COLD SEA TROUT

Cook a trout weighing from two to three lbs in court bouillon, and let it cool in the latter. Then drain it; sever the head and tail from the body, and put them aside. Completely skin the whole fish, and carefully separate the two fillets from the bones.

Deck each fillet with tarragon and chervil leaves, lobster coral, poached white of eggs, etc., and set them, back to back, upon a mousse of tomatoes lying in a special, long white or coloured porcelain dish about one and one-half to two inches deep.

Replace the head and tail, and cover the whole with a coating of half-melted, succulent fish aspic, somewhat clear. Let the aspic set, and encrust the dish containing the trout in a block of ice, or surround it with the latter broken.

A. Escoffier, *A Guide to Modern Cookery*, 1926

Sea Trout, Belle-Vue

Take a sea trout of the size required (the best are about two and a half to three pounds in weight, large enough for six to eight people). Put it in a court bouillon at the boiling point and poach it about twenty minutes.

Drain it well, remove the skin and put it in a long metal dish. Usually two sauces are served, a mayonnaise and a sauce verte.

The fish is surrounded by various trimmings.

These consist of hard-boiled eggs cut in half; the yolk is removed, mashed with butter, well seasoned and the cavity filled with this mixture. Others are filled with caviar. Tomatoes cut in half are scooped out and filled with either Russian salad or sardine butter; fonds d'artichauts or slices of poached cucumber can be treated in the same manner, but it is not advisable to use anchovies as one of the ingredients for the filling; the flavour is too strong and would kill the delicate taste of the fish.

Sea Trout with Cream

Take a sea trout about two pounds in weight and clean it well. Remove the skin carefully, and dip the fish in fresh cream, then in very little flour.

Put it in a long fireproof dish well buttered, cook it in a moderate oven a few minutes, then turn it on the other side.

Add then two glasses of sherry (or of dry white wine), let it reduce a while in a slower oven, basting well; a few minutes later add a good glass of fresh cream and finish the cooking, basting often.

Serve in the same dish.

The whole of the cooking takes a little less than half an hour, and you require about half a pint of cream for a two pound fish.

This excellent dish is garnished with little pieces of cucumber, cut olive shape and all the same size, cooked in salted water with a little butter in it, till soft, disposed either all round or in heaps at both ends of the dish. They should be particularly well drained so as not to spoil the cream sauce.

(A cook not used to that type of dish will find it easier to start cooking the trout with just butter for a few minutes; it will make the peeling easier. Then proceed with the recipe.)

Elvia and Maurice Firuski (eds), *The Best of Boulestin*, 1952

Revenge

Enjoy thy stream, thou little fish,
And should some angler for his dish
Through gluttony's vile sin
Attempt—the wretch—to pull thee out
God give thee strength, thou little trout,
To pull the rascal in.

Peter Pindar, quoted by Rose Henniker Heaton
in *The Perfect Hostess*, 1931

Trout

I CAUGHT my first trout in a burn in Inverness-shire. No more than two ounces apiece, with a dozen or so in my fishing bag at the end of each expedition, I would run home with boyish excitement to show them to my mother.

The best fish are those caught oneself and eaten within an hour or two. The baby trout were no exception. Wrapped in oatmeal, curling up in the frying pan like whitebait, never were fish more delicious.

Small trout have a sweetness and delicacy which their larger brethren cannot match. They are an exception to the general rule that pink or red flesh is preferable to white, for the fingerlings are almost invariably white. Frying is the only way to cook them; any other way would impair the flavour, and a sauce would destroy it. I should like, I admit, to try the Nowegian recipe for baked burn trout, but I fear I shall wait indefinitely before I ever have a surplus beyond what is needed for the frying pan.

As for court bouillon and sauces, Pollard was surely being cynical when he said that ninety-nine per cent of trout caught were not in perfect condition. It was a harsh judgement in 1926 when he wrote, but nowadays the fact that nearly all trout on the fishmonger's slab are of the rainbow variety, artificially reared, has made the precept more valid. Good though they may be, they are candidates for more than plain cooking. That principle applies to a wild trout too, if he be a pound or so in weight.

Ancients' Neglect

That this common fish has escaped the notice of all the ancients, except Ausonius (who celebrates it more for its beauty than fine flavour), is . . . matter of surprise; nor is it less singular, that so delicate a species should be neglected at a time when the folly and extravagance of the tables was at its height, and that the Epicures should overlook a fish that is found in such quantities in their neighbouring lakes, when they ransacked the Universe for dainties.

The Rev. W. B. Daniel, *Rural Sports*, 1807

Unwearied Appetite

It has been remarked by many other people, as well as myself, that, of all fish in existence, there is not one that you can partake of so many days in succession, without ceasing to enjoy it, as a trout, provided it be fresh caught, and well in season.

Lt-Col. P. Hawker, *Instructions to Young Sportsmen*, 1814.

Sub Jove

It was my first day's fishing on Lake Taupo in New Zealand, and after a morning spent vainly in trying to catch a trout with a dry imitation of a small blue dragon-fly, of which hundreds were coquetting in the sunlight, my boatman trailed a spoon and very quickly caught a 4 lb rainbow. We landed for lunch, and the man produced a folding gridiron, lit a fire of driftwood, got the billy going for tea, and by the time this was ready, the fire was in good fettle for the gridiron.

The trout was split open, dusted with salt and pepper, clasped in the grid, and set to cook on the red-hot embers, finishing with the skin down, so that none of the juice might be wasted. (This is very important in cooking fish thus.)

Sir Francis Colchester-Wemyss, *The Pleasures of the Table*, 1931

The Best Trout

The best trout are those whose flesh is red; in the Erne at Beleek, the trout are often redder than the salmon, and are in every way entirely commendable; some lochs also produce very red fish. White-fleshed trout may be served with more elaborate sauces . . .

Wyndham Forbes, *Salmon Fishing*, 1931

Institution of the St Ronan's Culinary Club

"Sir," said he [Dr Redgill], "I should not be surprised if they possessed the original receipt—a local one, too, I am told—for dressing the red trout, in this hereditary house of entertainment."

"Never doubt it, man,—claret, butter, and spiceries— Zounds, I have eat of it till—It makes my mouth water yet. As the French adage goes,—"Give your trout a bottle of good wine, a lump of butter, and spice, and tell me how you like him."

Margaret Dods, *The Cook & Housewife's Manual*, 1870 edition

To Tell Freshness

The newness or staleness . . . is known by the colour of their gills, their being hard or easy to be opened, the standing out or sinking of their eyes, their fins being stiff or limber, and by smelling to their gills.

Hannah Glasse, *The Art of Cooking Made Plain & Easy*, 1796

Packing to Send Away

Trout are probably at their best in April. They are then what the French call *saumounée*, a word which is preferable to the English equivalent "salmony". In theory, trout do not travel well enough to be sent as a gift to people who would really appreciate them, but in practice, if you want to send a dish of trout, they will travel well on most railways (I have mental reservations about the Southern) if wrapped in good newspaper. Dead fish have no preference, or even views on preference, but, *apart* from the political bias, they seem to travel best in the *Times* or the *Morning Post*, two papers one can always get in a decent countryside. Trout packed in the *Daily Express* have, on the other hand, been known to arrive in a

state of incorruption. It is probably due to some little susceptibility
we cannot hope to understand.

H. B. C. Pollard, *The Sportsman's Cookery Book*, 1926

Packing to Send Away

Before you send trout on a journey, have them gutted and washed,
but leave the scales on, and let them be laid on their backs, and
closely packed in willow (not flag) baskets, and with either flags or
dry wheat straw. Packing in damp grass or rushes is apt to ferment,
and therefore liable to spoil your fish. Moreover, you should have
the baskets made long and shallow, in order to avoid, as much as
possible, laying the trout on each other. For the last hint I am
indebted to my old factotum, Mr Grove in Bond Street, whom,
not only for his fish, but for his honour and honesty, I consider as
No I among the fishmongers.

Lt-Col. P. Hawker, *Instructions to Young Sportsmen*, 1814

VIRTUE OF PLAIN COOKING

Good trout, like salmon, are less likely to pall when they are dressed
with severe and Arcadian simplicity. For permanent appreciation of a
plain dish, one should stick to boiling or frying, and that was the
opinion of Sir Humphrey Davy, who was as much the philosopher with
the fish-kettles as over his chemical furnaces. When he had just given
elaborate instructions as to the *al fresco* crimping of his salmon, he says
decidedly as to a noble trout, in answer to a question from the
inquisitive Physicus, who was always eager for instruction, "We will
have him fried." And at the dinner afterwards when he righteously
forbade Harvey Sauce for the salmon he only admitted for the trout a
little vinegar and mustard—in fact, the elements of an *à la Tartare*
without the onions.

FRIED

To fry small trout—clean, wash and dry—roll in flour, and fry in butter
or clarified dripping to a delicate brown and do not overdo. Use a
heated cloth to absorb the grease, and serve with frizzled parsley and

slices of lemon. With larger fish, rub with flour or oatmeal, and fry in a deep pan, immersing them in butter, clarified dripping, or lard, heated so that the fish shall neither be scorched nor stewed.

À LA GENEVOISE

Clean, but do not scale. Put a little court bouillon [see as for salmon, page 175] in a stew-pan with parsley roots, cloves, parsley, bay leaves, onions and a carrot. Stew for half an hour. Strain the liquor over the trout in a small fish pan with a glass of Madeira. When boiled drain and remove the scales; then put it in the pan with a little of the liquor. Make a thickening and add veal gravy or red wine; season with mushrooms, parsley and green onions. Stew till smooth. Strain the sauce over the dished fish, with squeeze of lemon, essence of anchovy and some mace.

. . . We must reiterate that a rich dressing . . . should only be used with trout that are either inferior or somewhat stale.

A. I. Shand, *The Cookery of the Trout*, 1898

BOILING FISH

The water should be well salted, until it is at least as salt as the sea, and will float a fresh egg easily. It is then brought to boil furiously. Drop them in the boiling liquid, which will thereby be put off the boil, and as soon as it boils again, or in about a minute push the pot to one side so that it merely simmers. Ten minutes will be found to be the correct time of cooking for a fish of about a pound in weight.

CURING MUDDY FLAVOUR

And from some waters even the best of fresh-water fish taste muddy and nasty. This, however, can be cured. Should the owner be the happy possessor of a clear stream welling out of its native chalk or limestone, or other suitable supply of running water in which the fish can be confined alive, twelve to twenty-four hours captivity therein will clean its flesh. But if not, the fish's mouth should be filled as full as possible with salt and hung in a cool place till next day; when the salt will be found to have melted and dripped through the fish into the bowl placed to receive it, and its flesh will be no longer muddy.

Wyndham Forbes, *Salmon Fishing*, 1931

With Sauce Beurre Noire

. . . Beurre Noire is sometimes a change to the palate. Melt butter in a saucepan and add a few sprigs of parsley. Boil down till it takes on a dark colour; then, standing well back from the stove, because it spits like blazes, add a tablespoonful of vinegar and a few very finely chopped capers. A milder variant is to pour the rendered butter over the fish and then add the vinegar.

H. B. C. Pollard, *The Sportsman's Cookery Book*, 1926

With Fennel

Butter a dish, and scatter a fine julienne of fennel in it. Lightly season your trout with salt and a touch of cayenne, lay them in the dish, moisten with white wine, cover and poach the fish gently. When they are cooked, skin them, and arrange them on the serving-dish. Reduce the cooking liquor, thicken it with butter, heighten the seasoning a little, and pour this sauce over the trout.

Blue Trout

The essential condition of this picturesque dish is that the fish should be alive. Stun them, clean them as quickly as possible, plunge them immediately into a boiling court-bouillon consisting only of salted water with plenty of vinegar in it.

For quarter-pound trout, poach for ten minutes on the side of the fire. Arrange them on a napkin with parsley round them, and serve separately melted butter and steamed or boiled potatoes.

Au Chablis

Make a court bouillon with chablis, and poach the trout gently in it. With this court bouillon, make a white fish jelly. First, for two quarts of the fumet, put two pounds of chopped up raw fish bones and trimmings in a buttered pan with two ounces of minced onion, several parsley stalks and a dozen peppercorns. Let this stew for a while with the lid on, then add a quart of white wine and a little over two and a half pints of water. Add a pinch of salt and boil gently for twenty-five minutes. Strain through a fine conical sieve.

Then add, for a pint and three-quarters of fumet, nine ounces of chopped or pounded whiting flesh; the white part of a leek and a few parsley stalks cut in small pieces; a white of an egg, and about three-quarters of an ounce of gelatine softened in cold water. Clarify in the usual way, and strain through a napkin. Decorate the trout with tarragon leaves, little sprigs of chervil, white or yolk of hard-boiled egg etc., and cover them deeply with the cold jelly.

Ambrose Heath, *Madame Prunier's Fish Cookery Book*, 1938

To Bake Small Burn Trout (A Norwegian Recipe)

Lay your trout on his side upon a board, and with a very sharp knife cut right down to the bone just below the head. Then pass the blade below the bone and carefully remove it, snip off the fins with a pair of scissors, and put the two fillets at the bottom of a pie dish. When the first layer is complete cover it with butter, bay leaves, a little vinegar, and seasoning to taste, and make more layers until the dish is almost full. Fill up with water, and then bake in an oven. The result comes out in the form of a cake, and makes a delicious cold dish for breakfast or lunch.

A. E. Gathorne-Hardy, *My Happy Hunting Grounds*, 1914

Hell Fire Trout

Clean and prepare a large trout. Work together butter, finely chopped parsley, chives, a speck of garlic, mushrooms, two shallots, and basil, adding salt and coarsely ground pepper. Put the mixture inside the trout. The fish must then be placed in a pan just long enough to hold it, together with a carrot, a leek, and an onion stuck with three cloves.

Pour over it a mixture of white and red wines (two-thirds white and one-third red). This should rise two thumbs deep above the trout. Cook over a very fierce flame. When the liquid is boiling fiercely, set light to it with a piece of burning paper, and cook until the wine is almost the consistency of a sauce. Take out the vegetables, add a good piece of butter to the wine, season and serve the fish very hot.

André L. Simon (from *Manuel de Friandise*, 1796), *Fish*, 1940

À L'Auvergnate

Clean the trout, cut them across here and there, and dry them in a cloth, sprinkled lightly with flour. Melt a good piece of butter in the pan, and when at the foaming stage put in the trout. Cook them well on both sides.

Just before serving throw in a little shallot, onion and parsley, finely chopped. Having cooked it one minute add this to a sauce made as follows: Yolk of an egg in which you stir olive oil (as for a mayonnaise), vinegar, lemon juice, salt and pepper.

Put the fish in a serving dish and cover with the sauce.

Elvia and Maurice Firuski (eds), *The Best of Boulestin*, 1952

À la Montagnarde

Clean the fish for an hour in cold water. Then boil it on a brisk fire in a pan in which you have poured a bottle of hock or moselle with three onions, a bouquet of herbs, six cloves, a very little eschalot—garlic is the true thing—a few bay leaves and some butter well worked up with flour. Take out the onions and herbs and serve the fish in the remainder of the liquor, adding some scalded parsley.

Georgiana, Countess of Dudley, *The Dudley Book of Cookery & Household Recipes*, 1910

Trout with Wine (a Russian Dish)

Ingredients. 6 or 8 small trout, 1 tumbler of white wine, half a tumbler of Madeira, 1 wineglass of rum, 1 stick of celery, 1 small leek, 2 onions, bayleaf, mixed herbs, fish stock, salt and peppercorns.

Method. Put the trout in an earthenware casserole, cover with the different wines and a little fish stock, adding the vegetables and seasoning. Let them stand in this marinade for several hours. Then bring slowly to the boil and simmer for a few minutes till the fish is tender. Small trout, cooked in this way, will be found to be tender as soon as the marinade comes to the boil. These can be served either hot or cold, with a little of the marinade strained over them. When served hot, they are usually garnished with cooked crayfish, boiled potatoes and parsley.

À LA CATALANE

Ingredients. The number of trout required or 1 large trout, 1 or 2 onions, 1 clove of garlic, parsley, butter, vinegar, cumin, slices of lemon.

Method. The trout should be filleted, and if a large trout is used it should also be filleted, and the pieces subdivided. The fish is fried and then added to the following sauce, in which it should simmer for 5 minutes: Pound the garlic and parsley in a mortar, add the cumin, a little butter, and dissolve with a little water and vinegar. Put in a saucepan or deep frying pan, on a very slow fire, add the fish and the onions, previously fried to a golden colour in oil. For serving, pour the sauce over the fish and onions and garnish with slices of lemon.

À L'ESPAGNOLE

This curious recipe is very probably a survival of Moorish influence on Spanish food, as the use of honey with meat and fish dishes is common, both in African and Eastern cookery.

Ingredients. A few small trout, 4 or 5 shallots, 4 or 5 small mushrooms, 1 tablespoon of chopped chives, 1 or 2 tablespoons of honey, 1 glass of white wine, oil, a sprinkling of cumin, chopped parsley, salt and pepper.

Method. Put the fish in a casserole with the oil, the wine, the honey and the chopped shallots, and season with cumin, salt and pepper. Let the fish stand in this marinade for about an hour, then take them out, wrap each fish in a piece of plain foolscap paper, well oiled, place them in an earthenware casserole and cook on a very slow fire till tender. When ready, remove from the paper, put on a hot dish and serve with a butter sauce.

Countess Morphy, *Recipes of All Nations*, c. 1930

Pike

LOCH RANNOCH abounds with pike, as I discovered to my cost when my school was evacuated from Kent to Rannoch Lodge in 1940. Our rations were supplemented by the catching of numerous monster fish in wire cage traps at the mouth of the River Gaur, which flows into the loch. I do not recall, if indeed I ever knew, how they were cooked, but other than the fact that they took the edge off a youthful appetite, I do not look back on the experience with much pleasure.

Many years later, when our children were small, a French au pair girl introduced us to quenelles de brochet. What a revelation! I doubt if much can be done with big fish, but the dressing is the thing to make small pike exquisite.

Parson's Roast

May 16, 1781. Between 7 & 8 o'clock this morning went down to the River a fishing with my Nets . . . The largest Fish we caught was a Pike, which was a yard long and weighed upwards of thirteen pound.

May 17. I gave my Company for dinner my great Pike which was rosted and a Pudding in his Belly, some boiled Trout, Perch, and Tench, Eel and Gudgeon fryed, a Neck of Mutton boiled and a plain Pudding for Mrs Howes. I never saw a nobler Fish at any table, it was very well cooked, and tho' so large was declared by all the Company to be prodigious fine eating, being so moist.

Rev. James Woodforde, *Diary of a Country Parson, 1758–1802*

Preparation

The pike, like the perch, needs liquid and butter to supplement his scant supply of natural juices, and the liquid should be made from fish stock.

The angler landing a suitable pike should decide at once whether he means to eat him or not, for the fish if meant for the table should be cut at the gills and the tail immediately after it has been knocked on the head, then gutted and allowed to bleed as much as possible, a little proceeding which eliminates much of the sharp reedy flavour.

H. B. C. Pollard, *The Sportsman's Cookery Book*, 1926

The Trojan Horse

Do you know how to dress it? Roast or bake it of course; but the pudding—what of that? The ancients had a celebrated dish called the Trojan Horse. The horse was personated by a pig, and the Greeks in the inside by small poultry and delicacies of every imaginable kind, animal and vegetable. At the first gash of the carver, out rushed the thrushes and larks and truffles, etc. Your Trojan Horse is the jack, and the Greeks are to be personated by some oysters and some full brown mushrooms chopped small, and perhaps a little bacon, together with the other ordinary ingredients of a pudding . . .

Records of the Houghton Fishing Club, 1845. Letter of Henry Warburton to Canon Beadon. Quoted by W. Shaw Sparrow, *Angling in British Art*, 1923

Importance of Being in Season

Much depends on the pike being in season. After the spawning in the spring it loses colour and substance, the flesh becomes flabby, and for a time it is absolutely uneatable. It comes slowly into condition again with the warmth of the summer, and is at its best in the fall of the year or even in the early winter.

To Cook a Large Pike

If you have a great fish and mean to make the best of him, Mr Cholmondeley-Pennell's experience makes an excellent suggestion in his volume on Fishing in the Badminton Library:

"Another good way of treating large pike is to boil them and let them get cold, when the flesh, or rather fish, will break up easily into flakes, which when fried with a little fresh butter, plenty of pepper and salt (added continually whilst frying), and dredged over with flour or oatmeal, will be found to make a capital dish."

A Good Scotch Recipe for Stuffing and Baking

Having scaled and cleaned the fish, stuff with a maigre forcemeat, made thus: beat yolks of eggs, a few oysters bearded and chopped, and two boned anchovies, pounded biscuit or grated bread, minced parsley and a bit of eschalot or onion, pounded mace, black pepper, allspice and salt. Mix in the proper proportions, and having beat a good piece of butter in a stewpan, stir them in it over the fire till of the consistence of a thick butter. Fill the fish and sew up the slit. Bake in a moderate oven, basting with plenty of butter. Serve with anchovy sauce.

A. I. Shand, *The Cookery of the Pike & the Perch*, 1900

To Roast a Pike

. . . I am certain this direction how to roast him when he is caught is choicely good; for I have tried it, and it is somewhat the better for not being common. But with my direction you must take this caution, that your Pike must not be a small one, that is, it must be more than half a yard, and should be bigger.

First, open your Pike at the gills, and if need be, cut also a little slit towards the belly. Out of these, take his guts; and keep his liver, which you are to shred very small, with thyme, sweet marjoram, and a little winter-savoury; to these put some winter pickled oysters, and some anchovies, two or three; both these last whole, for the anchovies will melt, and the oysters should not; to these, you must add also a pound of sweet butter which you are to mix with the herbs that are shred, and let them all be well salted. If the Pike be more than a yard long, then you may put into there herbs more than a pound, or if he be less, then less butter will suffice: These, being thus mixt, with a blade or two of mace, must be put into the Pike's belly; and then his belly so sewed up as to keep all the butter in his belly if it be possible; if not, then as much of it as you possibly can. But take not off the scales. Then you are to thrust the spit through his mouth, out at his tail. And then take four or five or six split sticks, or very thin laths, and a convenient quantity of tape or filleting; these laths are to be tied round about the Pike's body from his head to his tail, and the tape tied somewhat thick, to prevent his breaking or falling off from the spit. Let him be roasted very leisurely; and often basted with claret wine, and anchovies, and butter, mixt together; and also with what moisture falls from him into the pan. When you have roasted him sufficiently, you are to hold under him, when you unwind or cut the tape that ties him, such a dish as you purpose to eat him out of; and let him fall into it with the sauce that is roasted in his belly; and by this means the Pike will be kept unbroken and complete. Then, to the sauce which was within, and also that sauce in the pan, you are to add a fit quantity of the best butter, and to squeeze the juice of three or four oranges. Lastly you may either put into the Pike, with the oysters, two cloves of garlick, and take it whole out, when the Pike is cut off the spit; or, to give the sauce a haut goût, let the dish into which you let the Pike fall be rubbed with it: The using or not using of the garlick is left to your discretion.

This dish of meat is too good for any but anglers, or very honest men; and I trust you will prove both, and therefore I have trusted you with this secret.

Izaak Walton, *The Compleat Angler*, 1653

─────────────── Pike Pudding ───────────────

Flake up the cold remains of a cooked pike into convenient pieces. Line a buttered pudding basin with suet crust, put in the fish with a piece of butter, three ounces of small mushrooms, a chopped shallot, capers and parsley. Add two sliced hard-boiled eggs, salt and pepper. (A few bearded sauce oysters chopped make a pleasant addition but are not necessary.) Fill up with well-flavoured fumet. Put on the suet crust, and boil for two and a half hours.

Serve with Sorrel sauce.

────────────── PIKE PASTIES ──────────────

Flake the remains of a cold cooked pike with a fork into small pieces. Mix it with a little mashed baked potato, two ounces of melted butter, one teaspoonful each of chopped parsley, chives and fennel, two minced shallots, the chopped yolks of two hard-boiled eggs, and two boned, minced anchovies, or a little anchovy essence, and pepper to taste. Bind the blended ingredients with Béchamel sauce.

Make, and cut out some rounds of pastry about four inches across. Put about two ounces of the prepared mixture on half of each circle of pastry and moisten the edges with water. Fold over the remaining half of pastry and seal the edges. Gild the pasties with beaten egg, and bake for about twenty minutes in a 400 degree oven.

Note. Cheese pastry is very suitable for these pasties. In the mixing, add finely grated cheddar and a little pepper to the flour, salt and fat. Fumet, too, may be used instead of water for moistening the dough if liked.

Margaret Butterworth, *Now Cook Me The Fish*, 1950

────────────── FRIED FILLETS ──────────────

The principle of filleting is good, not only as a disguise, and it cannot be denied that the pike is not an attractive dish to the eye, but also because when you have cut fillets off him, the remains can be rapidly stewed up to form a fish bouillon or gravy as a basis for the sauce with which you eat the fillets.

To proceed: cut your fillets, stew the remains for an hour with a sliced onion or shallots, spices, herbs, and lemon, reduce, then add butter and flour and a dash of anchovy, stirring the whole to a cream sauce. Harvey's or Worcester may be sparingly added if desired, but it is not wise to make the sauce too piquant, unless doubt is felt that the pike be too fishy in flavour. Egg and breadcrumb the fillets, get the frying mixture very hot, and fry quickly till properly browned.

H. B. C. Pollard, *The Sportsman's Cookery Book*, 1926

PIKE QUENELLES

These quenelles are made with ordinary pike forcemeat, but they are better if it is a mousseline forcemeat. Mould them with a dessertspoon, and place them as they are moulded on a buttered shallow fireproof dish or a sauté-pan. Cover them with boiling salted water and poach them. They are done as soon as the forcemeat feels firm to the touch. Drain them on a cloth, arrange them in a circle on the serving-dish, and pour the chosen sauce in the middle.

MOUSSELINE FORCEMEAT

Pound finely a pound of pike with nearly half an ounce of salt, a pinch of white pepper and the whites of three small eggs added by degrees. Pass through a fine tammy-cloth, put the forcemeat into a basin and keep it on ice for an hour. Then, still on the ice, work into it by small degrees a pint of good cream.

Ambrose Heath, *Madame Prunier's Fish Cookery Book*, 1938

Eel

EELS do not rank as game fish, but they are under-rated and should be on the repertoire of any country kitchen where they may be caught locally. Their unpopularity stems from their alien, serpentine appearance, and from the difficulty of skinning them.

Small, succulent, freshwater eels are caught in our lochs with a worming rod, and are generally between 15 & 18 inches in length. Once skinned, they are cut into two-inch sections and grilled or fried in oatmeal or flour. In flavour and texture they emulate a young trout similarly cooked.

Eels are plentiful in Scottish lochs and rivers, but unlike the dwellers by Thames or Severn the Scots view them with dislike or indifference. Smoked eel is an exception, for that has become popular as an alternative to smoked salmon. Simple, but rather rich, it should be served with brown bread and butter and slices of lemon.

In the interests of freshness, those who buy eels from a fishmonger should ask to see them alive. Then, once killed, the fishmonger will skin them. For the fisher of eels instruction is necessary in this esoteric task. The best way to kill an eel is to behead it with a sharp knife, and this makes the subsequent task of skinning easier. The metaphor, slippery as an eel, is apt, and that is what makes it seem difficult. My own method, quite sir..ply, is to wrap the eel in a piece of cloth and lay it gently in a vice. Next, with a sharp knife I make an incision about an inch long down its back. The circle of skin is then drawn back with a pair of pliers and, once it begins to move, it may be drawn off the whole body like a glove.

FRIED

First kill, then skin, empty, and wash them as clean as possible; cut them into four-inch lengths, and dry them well in a soft cloth. Season them with fine salt, and white pepper, or cayenne, flour them thickly, and fry them a fine brown in boiling lard; drain and dry them . . . and send them to table with plain melted butter or anchovy sauce. Eels are sometimes dipped into batter and then fried; or into egg and fine breadcrumbs (mixed with minced parsley or not, at pleasure), and served with plenty of crisped parsley round, and on them.

It is an improvement for these modes of dressing the fish to open them entirely; and remove the bones: the smaller parts should be thrown into the pan a minute or two later than the thicker portions of the bodies or they will not be equally done.

Eliza Acton, *Modern Cookery for Private Families*, 1845

TO ROAST STUFFED EEL ON A SPIT

It is agreed by most men, that the Eel is a most dainty fish: the Romans have esteemed her the Helena of their feasts; and some the queen of palate-pleasure.

First, wash him in water and salt; then pull off his skin below his vent or navel, and not much further: having done that, take out his guts as clean as you can, but wash him not: then give him three or four Scotches with a knife; and then put into his belly and those scotches, sweet herbs, an anchovy, and a little nutmeg grated or cut very small, and your herbs and anchovies must also be cut very small; and mixt with good butter and salt: having done this, then pull his skin over him, all but his head which you are to cut off, to the end you may tie his skin about that part where his head grew, and it must be so tied as to keep all his moisture within his skin: and having done this, tie him with tape or packthread to a spit, and roast him leisurely; and baste him with water and salt till his skin breaks, and then with butter; and, having roasted him enough, let what was put into his belly, and what he drips, be his sauce.

Izaac Walton, *The Compleat Angler*, 1653

Au Vert

. . . There is a Belgian recipe which is simple and extraordinarily good. Skin your eels by cutting an incision round the neck, holding the head down with a two-pronged fork and stripping the skin away like a glove to the tail. Then slightly grill or roast, so that the oil comes out. Wipe down with a cloth (this eliminates the sometimes too strong flavour and muddiness of eels). Chop them in pieces about 3 inches long, and add half the quantity of chopped sorrel to which a liberal proportion of parsley, chervil, mint, and herbs have been added. Cook it all together with a piece of butter the size of a nut for about a quarter of an hour and fairly fast, then add a wineglassful of white wine or a sparing dash of lemon-juice.

In general, eels should be cooked in a "court bouillon" of white wine, bay-leaf, onion, carrot, clove and chopped parsley. If desired, they can be served like this as plain stewed eel, or they can be set aside, cooled, egg and breadcrumbed, fried, and served with a Tartare sauce. Cold jellied eel set in a white-wine jelly of its own juice is ideal. Should the supply of eels be inadequate and difficulty be experienced in getting a sauce thick enough to set, it can be reinforced with isinglass, *not* gelatine, or by fish stock made of other fish. When in doubt as to whether the eels may be muddy, let them soak in salt water for a day, and change the water several times.

H. B. C. Pollard, *The Sportsman's Cookery Book*, 1926

Matelote of Eel

Put into a stew-pan some onion, carrot, thyme, bay leaf, parsley and a little garlic. Mix in sufficient butter to parboil. Then add half a pint of white wine. When this is ready to boil put into it the pieces of eel to cook. Make a brown butter sauce, add it to the eel liquor and let it all boil for three or four hours, being careful to skim it well. Just before serving fry golden coloured in butter some very small onions and also some small white mushrooms. The pieces of eel should only cook for fifteen minutes.

Georgiana, Countess of Dudley, *The Dudley Book of Cookery & Household Recipes*, 1910

—————————————— Eels Bourguignonne ——————————————

Prepare a roux with a piece of butter the size of a small egg, and the same quantity of flour; let it get slightly brown.

Take a pint of red wine and bring it to the boil. Season it with salt, pepper, a bouquet of parsley, thyme and bay leaf and one fillet of anchovy, finely chopped. Add a dozen button onions, previously cooked in butter.

Let the wine reduce by a quarter and put in the pieces of eel (about three inches long); cook slowly for about twenty minutes.

Make a sauce by adding the wine stock, little by little, to the roux you have prepared. Stir well, seeing that it is smooth and about the consistency of cream.

Dispose the pieces of eel (well drained and kept hot) in the serving dish, finish the sauce by adding to it a few pieces of butter off the fire, pour all over the fish and garnish with fried croûtons. Some people add a few prunes, stoned and cut in half.

Elvia & Maurice Firuski (eds), *The Best of Boulestin*, 1952

—————————————— Eel Mould ——————————————

Make some fish jelly with a court-bouillon of the trimming of gelatinous fish and some good white braising liquor. Cut up in pieces the requisite number of eels, and let them marinate with finely chopped carrot and onion, garlic, parsley stalks, thyme and bay leaf, lemon juice, white port and a little brandy, for an hour. Then cook them in the prepared jelly to which you add the marinade. Cook very gently for an hour. Drain the pieces of eel, remove the bones and any uneatable parts. Pass the cooking liquor through a sieve, and reduce it. Now take a rectangular mould, and arrange in it the eel fillets in layers, alternating them with layers of a large amount of chopped parsley, which has been blanched, plunged in cold water, and then pressed dry, so that between each layer of eel there is a strip of green. Finally pour the reduced cooking liquor into the mould, and let it get cold in a cool place. (All grease will of course have first been removed from the cooking liquor). To serve, turn the mould out, cut it in slices, and serve them on a napkin with green salad round them.

Ambrose Heath, *Madame Prunier's Fish Cookery Book*, 1938

─────────── COLLARED EELS ───────────

One rather large eel   Salted water
A little powdered mace   2 tablespoons vinegar
A little allspice   Few leaves sage
2 cloves   Few sprigs parsley
Salt & pepper   Lemon slices to garnish

Cut the eel into chunks; bone it but do not remove skin. Rub the interior with the ground spices mixed with salt and pepper and roll up tightly, fastening with strong tape. The fish may, if preferred, be left whole. Cook in salted water to which vinegar has been added. Allow to cool and pickle in the water; the sage and parsley may be added when boiling, or the French method of preparing a court bouillon may be adopted and the fish cooked in this and allowed to cool in it. Remove tape and serve with slices of lemon and parsley to garnish.

─────────── JELLIED EELS ───────────

Cut up the required number of eels into chunks and let these marinate overnight in a white wine court-bouillon, with the usual vegetables, bay leaf and thyme. Boil gently for a long time the trimmings of mackerel, herrings, or any other oily fish with bones and, if available, a cow's heel. You will thus get a fish jelly, and you will cook in it the chunks of eel, together with their wine marinade, for an hour or longer. Drain the pieces of eel; remove bone and skin. Pass through a sieve the liquor in which the eels were cooked, simmer a little longer to reduce it, and then pour over the eel in a deep dish or pot, after having carefully removed all surface fat. Let it get quite cold and serve.

André L. Simon, *Fish*, 1940

─────────── EELS À LA FLORENTINE (ITALIAN) ───────────

Ingredients. 2 lbs of eel, oil, 2 cloves of garlic, 2 or 3 bay leaves, breadcrumbs, salt and pepper.

Method. Skin the eel and cut in 2 inch lengths. Put a little oil in a pie dish with the chopped garlic and the bay leaves and, when hot, add the pieces of eel, coated with breadcrumbs. Moisten with a little more oil. Season with salt and pepper, and bake till the pieces of eel are slightly brown and quite tender. Add 1 or 2 tablespoons of water in the course of baking.

Countess Morphy, Recipes of All Nations, c. 1930

HAMBURG EEL SOUP

Skin and cut up an eel, sprinkle it with salt and let it lie an hour or so. Meanwhile cook in a quart of good stock for half an hour a small head of celery, a carrot, half a pint of shelled green peas and a bouquet of parsley, thyme and sage. Thicken this with a tablespoonful each of butter and flour. Peel also half a pound of small pears and stew them in white wine with lemon peel and sugar. When they are done, drain them, and put them in the tureen to keep warm. Now boil the pieces of eel for a quarter of an hour in three-quarters of a pint of salted water with a few peppercorns, and then add the pieces with the strained liquor they were boiled in to the vegetable soup. Boil it up, squeeze half a lemon into it, strain again, thicken it with the yolks of three eggs and pour it on the tops of pears, serving with the pieces of eel in it.

EEL BROTH

Fry a sliced medium-sized onion in dripping or butter until brown, add three pints of stock or water, a skinned eel cut up, bring to the boil, skim and simmer for about an hour. Twenty minutes before serving, strain the broth and put it back into the pan, season with pepper and salt and sprinkle in a tablespoonful of crushed sago or tapioca. At the last minute put in a little chopped parsley and serve with the pieces of eel in it.

Ambrose Heath, Good Soups, 1935

Epitaph

God grant that I may fish
Until my dying day.
And when it comes to my last cast,
I humbly pray.
When in the Lord's landing net
I'm peacefully asleep
That in his mercy
I be judged as good enough to keep.

Charles John Fitzroy Rhys Wingfield,
in Great Barrington Church, Oxfordshire.

Bibliography

Acton, Eliza, *Modern Cookery for Private Families*, 1845.

Allen, M. L., *Savoury Dishes for Breakfast*, J. S. Virtue & Co., London, 1886.

Astley, Sir John, *Fifty Years of My Life*, Hurst & Blackett, London, 1894.

The Badminton Magazine.

Mrs Beeton, *All-About Cookery*, Ward, Lock & Co. Limited, London, c. 1930.

Boulestin, *The Best of Boulestin* (Ed: Elvia & Maurice Firuski), William Heinemann, London, 1952.

Brand, Margery, *Fifty Ways of Cooking Game in India*, Thacker, Spink & Co. (1933) Ltd, Calcutta, 1942.

Brillat-Savarin, Jean-Anthelme, *The Philosopher in the Kitchen*, translated by Anne Drayton, Penguin Books, Harmondsworth, 1970.

Butterworth, Margaret, *Now Cook Me The Fish*, Country Life Ltd, London, 1950.

Cameron, Allan Gordon, *The Wild Red Deer of Scotland*, William Blackwood & Sons, Edinburgh & London, 1923.

Chalmers, Patrick R., *At The Sign of The Dog & Gun*, Philip Allan & Co. Ltd, London, 1930.

Chalmers, Patrick R., *Deerstalking*, Philip Allan, London, 1935.

Chalmers, Patrick, *The Shooting Man's England*, Seeley Service & Company Ltd, London, c. 1930.

Chaytor, A. H., *Letters to a Salmon Fisher's Sons*, John Murray, London, 1910.

Colchester-Wemyss, Sir Francis, *The Pleasures of the Table*, James Nisbet & Co. Ltd, London, 1931.

Colquhoun, John, *The Moor and the Loch*, William Blackwood & Sons, Edinburgh & London, 1888 (first published 1840).

Conway, James, *Forays among Salmon & Deer*, Chapman & Hall, London, 1861.

Daniel, The Reverend W. B., *Rural Sports*, Longman, Hurst, Rees & Orme, London, 1807.

Dickens, Charles, *The Pickwick Papers*, 1836.

Dods, Margaret, *The Cook & Housewife's Manual*, Oliver & Boyd, Edinburgh, 1870 (originally published 1826).

Dudley, Georgiana, Countess of, *The Dudley Book of Cookery & Household Recipes*, Edward Arnold, London, 1910.

Dudley, Georgiana, Countess of, *A Second Dudley Book of Cookery*, Hutchinson & Co., London, 1914.

Edward, Second Duke of York, *The Master of Game* (Ed: W. A. & F. Baillie-Grohman), Chatto & Windus, London, 1909 (first published c. 1410).

Egan, Pierce, *Sporting Anecdotes*, Sherwood, Jones & Co., London, 1820.

Escoffier, A., *A Guide to Modern Cookery*, William Heinemann, London, 1926.

Fairfax, Thomas, *The Complete Sportsman*, printed for J. Cooke, London, N.D.

Folkard, H. C., *The Wild-Fowler*, Longmans, Green, London, 1875.

Forbes, Wyndham, *Salmon Fishing*, Seeley, Service & Co. Ltd, London, 1931.

Fores's Sporting Notes and Sketches, Messrs Fores, London, 1898.

Fraser, Margaret, *A Highland Cookery Book*, John Lane, The Bodley Head, London, 1930.

Fur, Feather & Fin Series, Longmans, Green & Co., London.
  George Saintsbury, *The Grouse*, 1895
  George Saintsbury, *The Partridge*, 1894
  Alexander Innes Shand, *The Pheasant*, 1895
  Alexander Innes Shand, *Snipe & Woodcock*, 1904
  Alexander Innes Shand, *Ducks & Geese*, 1905
  Col. Kenney Herbert, *The Hare*, 1896
  Alexander Innes Shand, *The Rabbit*, 1898
  Alexander Innes Shand, *Venison*, 1896
  Alexander Innes Shand, *The Salmon*, 1898

Alexander Innes Shand, *Pike & Perch*, 1900

Alexander Innes Shand, *The Trout*, 1898.

Gathorne-Hardy, A. E., *My Happy Hunting Grounds*, Longmans, Green, London, 1914.

Glasse, Hannah, *The Art of Cookery Made Plain & Easy*, London, 1796.

Grimble, Augustus, *Deer-Stalking*, Chapman & Hall, London, 1888.

Grimble, Augustus, *Leaves from a Game Book*, Kegan Paul, Trench, Trubner & Co., London, 1898.

Grimble, Augustus, *More Leaves from My Game Book*, R. Clay & Sons, London, 1917.

Hardinge, Lord of Penshurst, *On Hill and Plain*, John Murray, London, 1933.

Hare, C. E., *The Language of Sport*, Country Life Limited, London, 1939.

Hawker, Lt-Col. P., *Instructions to Young Sportsmen*, Herbert Jenkins, London, 1922 (first published 1814).

Heath, Ambrose, *From Creel to Kitchen*, Adam & Charles Black, London, 1939.

Heath, Ambrose, *Good Poultry & Game Dishes*, Faber & Faber, London, 1953.

Heath, Ambrose, *Good Savouries*, Faber & Faber, London, 1934.

Heath, Ambrose, *Good Soups*, Faber & Faber, London, 1935.

Heath, Ambrose, *Madame Prunier's Fish Cookery Book*, Nicholson & Watson, London, 1938.

Heaton, Nell and Simon, André, *A Calendar of Food & Wine*, Faber and Faber, London, 1949.

Heaton, Rose Henniker, *The Perfect Hostess*, Methuen & Co. Ltd, London, 1931.

Herman, Senn, C., *The Art of the Table*, London, 1923.

Minnie, Lady Hindlip's Cookery Book, Thornton Butterworth, London, 1925.

Hooper, Mary, *Handbook for the Breakfast Table*, Griffith & Farran, London, 1873.

"Idstone", *The "Idstone" Papers*, Horace Cox, London, 1872.

Jeans, Thomas, *The Tommiebeg Shootings*, George Routledge & Sons, London, 1860.

Marshall, Mrs A. B., *Mrs. A. B. Marshall's Cookery Book*, Simpkin, Marshall, Hamilton, Kent & Co. Ltd, London, c. 1880.

"Martingale", *Sporting Scenes & Country Characters*, Longman, Orme, Brown, Green & Longmans, London, 1840.

Morphy, Countess, *Recipes of All Nations*, Herbert Joseph for Selfridge & Co. Ltd, London, c. 1930.

Murray, Hilda, *Echoes of Sport*, T. N. Foulis, London & Edinburgh, 1910.

Murrell, John, *Two Books of Cookerie & Carving*, printed for John Marriot, London, 1638.

Mackenzie, Osgood, *A Hundred Years in the Highlands*, Edward Arnold, London, 1924.

McNeill, F. Marian, *The Book of Breakfasts*, Alexander Maclehose & Co., London, 1932.

McNeill, F. Marian, *The Scots Kitchen*, Grafton Books, London, 1989 (first published 1929).

North, Christopher, *Noctes Ambrosianae*, Hamilton, Adams & Co., London, Thomas D. Morison, Glasgow, 1888.

Parker, Eric, *The Shooting Week-End Book*, Seeley Service & Co. Ltd, London, N.D.

Pollard, H. B. C., *The Gun Room Guide*, Eyre & Spottiswoode, London, 1930.

Pollard, H. B. C., *The Sportsman's Cookery Book*, Country Life Ltd, London, 1926.

Prichard, H. Hesketh, *Sport in Wildest Britain*, Philip Allan, London, N.D. (first published 1921).

de Salis, Mrs, *Entrées A La Mode*, Longmans, Green & Co., London, 1890.

Scott, Sir Walter, *Waverley*, 1814.

Scrope, William, *The Art of Deer Stalking*, John Murray, London, 1839.

Shand, Alexander Innes, *Shooting*, J. M. Dent & Co., London, 1902.

Simon, André L., *Fish*, The Wine & Food Society, London, 1940.

Simon, André L., *Food*, Burke Publishing Company, London, 1949.

Simon, André L., *The Art of Good Living*, Constable & Co. Ltd, London, 1930.

Smith, Henry, *The Master Book of Poultry & Game*, Spring Books, London, c. 1950.

Somerset, Susan, Duchess of, *The Duchess Cookery Book*, Grayson & Grayson, London, 1934.

Sparrow, W. Shaw, *Angling in British Art*, John Lane The Bodley Head, London, 1923.

Spencer, Edward, *Cakes & Ale*, Grant Richards, London, 1897.

The Sporting Magazine.

Surtees, R. S., *Mr Facey Romford's Hounds*, Bradbury, Agnew, London, 1865.

Thornhill, R. B., *The Shooting Directory*, Longman, Hurst, Rees & Orme, London, 1804.

Thornton, Thomas, *A Sporting Tour*, Edward Arnold, London, 1896 (first published 1804).

Venner, Dr Tobias, *Via recta ad vitam Longam*, London, 1628.

Walsh, J. H., F.R.C.S., *The British Cookery Book*, Routledge, Warne & Routledge, London, 1864.

Walsingham, Lord & Sir Ralph Payne-Gallwey, *Shooting: Moor & Marsh* (Badminton Library), Longmans, Green, London, 1887.

Walton, Izaak, *The Compleat Angler*, J. M. Dent & Sons Ltd, London, 1947 (first published 1653).

Williamson, D., *The Practice of Cookery & Pastry Adapted to the Business of Every-Day Life*, J. Menzies & Co., Edinburgh, 1884.

Woodforde, The Reverend James, *Diary of a Country Parson, 1758–1802*, Oxford University Press, London, 1935.

Yates, Lucy H., *The Country Housewife's Book*, Country Life Ltd, London, 1934.

Acknowledgements

The author and publisher would like to thank the following for permission to quote from copyright material:

The Best of Boulestin ed. Elvia and Maurice Firuski, William Heinemann.

The Perfect Hostess by Rose Henniker Heaton, Methuen.

Minnie, Lady Hindlip's Cookery Book, Butterworth.

The Gun Room Guide by H. B. C. Pollard, Eyre & Spottiswoode.

From Creel to Kitchen by Ambrose Heath, A. & C. Black.

On Hill and Plain by Lord Hardinge of Penshurst, John Murray.

The Art of Good Living by André Simon, Constable & Co.

A Highland Cookery Book by Margaret Fraser, John Lane, The Bodley Head.

Angling in British Art by W. Shaw Sparrow, John Lane, The Bodley Head.

Now Cook Me the Fish by Margaret Butterworth, Country Life.

The Language of Sport by C. E. Hare, Country Life.

The Sportsman's Cookery Book by H. B. C. Pollard, Country Life.

The Country Housewife's Book by Lucy H. Yates, Country Life.

The Philosopher in the Kitchen by Jean Anthelme Brillat-Savarin, translated by Anne Drayton, Penguin Books.

Food by André Simon, Burke Publishing.

Good Soups by Ambrose Heath, Faber & Faber.

Good Savouries by Ambrose Heath, Faber & Faber.

Good Poultry and Game Dishes by Ambrose Heath, Faber & Faber.

Index